332.6441 NEW
The secret financial
life of food : from commo
Newman, Kara
967868

LC OCT 2013

Ru Feb 17

SO OCT 2017

The Secret Financial Life of Food

Arts and Traditions of the Table: Perspectives on Culinary History

THE
SECRET
FINANCIAL LIFE
OF FOOD

From Commodities Markets to Supermarkets

Kara Newman

COLUMBIA UNIVERSITY PRESS

NEW YORK

Columbia University Press
Publishers Since 1893
New York   Chichester, West Sussex
cup.columbia.edu
Copyright © 2013 Columbia University Press
All rights reserved

Library of Congress Cataloging-in-Publication Data

Newman, Kara.
The secret financial life of food : from commodities markets to
supermarkets / Kara Newman.
p. cm. — (Arts and traditions of the table: perspectives on culinary history)
Includes bibliographical references and index.
ISBN 978-0-231-15670-7 (cloth : alk. paper)
ISBN 978-0-231-52734-7 (e-book)
1. Commodity exchanges—History.   2. Agriculture—Economic aspects—History.
3. Food—History.   I. Title.
HG6046.N49 2013
332.64′41—dc23
2012010138

Columbia University Press books are printed on permanent and durable acid-free paper.
This book is printed on paper with recycled content.
Printed in the United States of America

c 10 9 8 7 6 5 4 3 2 1

COVER ART: Lew Robertson, © Getty Images
COVER DESIGN: Milenda Nan Ok Lee

References to Internet Web sites (URLs) were accurate at the time of writing. Neither the author nor Columbia University Press is responsible for URLs that may have expired or changed since the manuscript was prepared.

To Eliott Newman and Naomi Newman

Contents

Acknowledgments

Bringing this book to life meant dealing with a number of hurdles, from lost historical archives to recalcitrant traders and close-lipped corporate gatekeepers. But a number of people were critical in helping to uncover resources, providing helpful and intelligent information, as well as support through the rougher patches. The following individuals are worth their weight in gold (or any other commodity they see fit to trade): Author and culinary historian extraordinaire Betty Fussell was instrumental in helping flesh out the early outline for this book and encouraging me to pursue it; her books *The Story of Corn* and *Raising Steaks* proved to be valuable resources. Culinary history powerhouse Andrew F. Smith provided endless encouragement, and I am honored to know him as teacher, historian, and friend. The Culinary Historians of New York, particularly Cathy Kaufman and Linda Pelaccio, who allowed me to present parts of the pork belly chapter to the membership, showed me that an audience for this book exists.

Since it is nearly impossible to persuade traders and corporations to reveal their trading activities, past or present, I relied on historical newspaper accounts to piece together some historical arcs. For that, I am indebted to New York University's Bobst Library, the New York Public Library's archives, and librarian Melody Allison of the Funk Family Agriculture,

Consumer, and Environmental Sciences Library at the University of Illinois, Urbana-Champaign.

It was a particular disappointment to learn just how much of the former New York Mercantile Exchange's historical archives were lost when the tragedy of September 11, 2001, decimated the exchange's home in the World Trade Center. However, a number of industry insiders, current and former, provided information that helped connect together stories, including Curt Zuckert at the CME Group, Lee Underwood and Tim Barry at the IntercontinentalExchange, and Will Acworth at the Futures Industry Association. I am particularly grateful that Leo Melamed, chairman emeritus of the Chicago Mercantile Exchange, and Joseph O'Neill, former president of the New York Cotton Exchange, granted interviews.

A number of finance and economics experts generously shared their time and expertise for this project: Alan Bush of Archer Financial Services, Chad Hart of Iowa State University, Bill G. Lapp of Advanced Economic Solutions, Ron Plain of the University of Missouri, and Jim Robb of the Livestock Marketing Information Center.

Gratitude also is due to Jennifer Sondag and Chris Grams of the CME Group for their gracious assistance in obtaining images to include in the book, as well as to Ryan Carlson, who maintains the fascinating Trading Pit Blog (www.tradingpitblog.com). Thank you also to culinary historian Lynne Olver for granting permission to reprint her useful and highly entertaining Hershey Bar Index.

The team at Columbia University Press deserves special mention, particularly editor extraordinaire Jennifer Crewe, as well as Jay Harward, Meredith Howard, Irene Pavitt, and Kathryn Schell.

Finally, I am lucky to have the following people in my corner: Sandra and Alan Silverman; Joelle, Laurie, and Rowana Miller; Jennifer and Madelyn Sendor; Naomi and Eliott Newman; and, especially, Robert Silverman.

The Secret Financial Life of Food

Introduction
Buy Breakfast

Few people can claim to have had a food epiphany while reading *Barron's*, but that's what happened to me. In a roundtable discussion of market experts, after many dry pages about where the S&P 500 Index and gold bullion might end the year, commodities trader Jim Rogers offered this wisdom: "Buy breakfast."

He was referring to futures contracts sold on frozen orange juice and pork bellies, which he expected to appreciate in value during the coming year. But to me, it was more than an investment idea. I thought of the BLTs and cartons of Tropicana orange juice I'd consumed over the years. Although I had a vague notion of the agriculture and manufacturing associated with bringing food to the table, never before had I contemplated the secret financial life of my meals.

At the time, I was working as a financial editor for a consulting firm, overseeing a team that churned out daily stock and bond market reports for corporate clients. I was given a new and serendipitous task: write a daily commodities report.

Suddenly, I was hungry on the commodities beat, and I wanted to learn more. I enrolled in a course on derivatives offered by the Futures Industry Institute and taught by a commodities trader. The class was geared toward prepping eager young traders for a certification exam. I flipped past the pages on interest rate futures and diagrams of hedging strategies to the list of products traded as commodities.

For the uninitiated, the commodities market generally is divided into five sectors: metals, energy, livestock, softs, and grains. The first two I found fairly straightforward: metals includes precious metals and base metals, such as copper and aluminum, while energy refers to products like crude oil and natural gas.

But after that, the course book read like a menu: The livestock category includes cattle (live cattle and feeder cattle) and hogs (live and the fabled "pork bellies," a commodity now ubiquitous on trendy restaurant menus but which ceased trading in 2011). The grains sector spans the range of corn, oats, soybeans, and wheat. And the softs group refers to cocoa, coffee, orange juice, sugar, and, puzzlingly, also cotton and lumber.

And that's just a partial list. It goes on, especially if you include contracts that are traded outside the United States and those that once traded here but are no longer: barley; butter and cheese; chickens; eggs, which surprisingly were a highly speculative market during the 1970s; fruit; milk; peppercorns—red, green, or black (largely traded in India, as are most other spices); potatoes; and rice. Apparently, if one can consume it, one can trade it.

How long had this been going on? A partial answer comes from *Harper's New Monthly Magazine*, describing the grain auctions that took place at the former New York Produce Exchange in lower Manhattan. "The Call Room daily presents an immense spectacle of the traffic in grain," the article says. A potential buyer might peer through a magnifying glass at a flour sample held in the palm of his hand, even tipping in water from "a handy little teapot" to judge its suitability for baking. The business of trading would commence at 10:30 A.M.: "William L. Eichell, caller of grain presides. In rapid, monotonous voice, drawn out at the close of each sentence, he announces: 'No. 2 oats, January. What are they offered at?' A seller, in loud, explosive tones, replies, 'At 34¾' (per bushel), or 'at ¾.' At '¾,' jerkily echoes the caller. 'What is bid? ⅛ bid, ¼, ½, ⅝ bid.' 'I'll take 'em,' shrieks an excited individual. 'Sold by Jones to Smith at ¾.'" Further lots would be sold in this manner. "The call lasts ten or fifteen minutes, and occasionally has the accompaniment of callithumpian discord, blended with the fiendish screeches of a dozen frenzied locomotives."[1]

The article includes a photo of the former Produce Exchange circa 1874, once housed at Two Broadway, now the site of a black marble-faced office building with art deco trim. At the time, the Produce Exchange was the nation's leading market in wheat, flour, lard, and cottonseed oil.

Today's trading process is considerably more antiseptic. Rows of flickering computer screens replace the tables piled high with flour and grains. However, the exchange setting remains as dramatic as its late-nineteenth-century counterpart: the maze of commodity pits ringed with traders in colorful jackets barking orders into phones or across the pit at one another, the carpet of paper tickets littering the floor, refuting the myth of the paperless office. But the physical commodities—the bushels of corn, the blocks and barrels of cheddar—are traded but are nowhere to be seen.

I began to follow the commodities market more closely. After only a few weeks of scrutinizing the ups and downs of the market, I was amazed by the fragility of the same commodities that sit so sturdily on the supermarket shelf. Take coffee, for example. Within the space of a few weeks, the price of coffee was buffeted by tropical storms and early frosts that threatened to crimp crop output. Then came an onslaught of a disease that threatened crops across much of Latin America, where the majority of coffee beans grow. The commodity price soared as a shortage was predicted. Finally, a wily spectator who had "cornered the market" unloaded mass quantities of coffee, driving prices back down. There was no run on jars of Folgers at the grocery. The price of my daily latte didn't fluctuate by even a penny. Nobody else seemed aware of the high drama—that the price of coffee had skyrocketed, that the crop had nearly been wiped out.

Yet, events of this magnitude happen every day and, over the long run, affect not only the commodities market but also the products on offer at the local supermarket. This is the story of the secret financial life of food— the history of how it all came to be, including where, how, and why our food is traded—a critical but nearly invisible connection between the farm and plate.

Chalk markers tally prices from various American and Canadian grain markets at the Chicago Board of Trade (early twentieth century). (Image used with the permission of CME Group Inc. © 2011. All rights reserved.)

CHAPTER ONE

How Does Commodities Trading Work?

What shall we eat, what shall we drink, and wherewithal
shall we be lighted? Are the three questions
with whose pleasant solution the . . . Exchange charges itself.
HARPER'S NEW MONTHLY MAGAZINE, JULY 1886

This is not a book on how to trade commodity futures; it is a book about culinary history and the role that the commodities market has played in shaping culinary history. But before delving into the histories of the various contracts, it is important first to address three questions: How did the commodities market evolve into what we know today? How does the modern commodities market work? And perhaps most important, how does the trading of food-based commodities influence what we eat and what we pay for food?

The Evolution of the Commodities Market

Though it is impossible to put a time stamp on the very first commodities market transaction, many traders like to point out that the concept of grain "futures" dates all the way back to the days of the Hebrew Bible: Joseph analyzed the pharaoh's dream of cattle and crops, discerned that a drought would come, and diligently went about storing immense amounts of grain. By the time the famine arrived, Joseph had cornered the grain market, ultimately becoming a very rich man.

Others pinpoint the birth of the markets as taking place in Osaka, Japan, in 1730. Feudal lords there established warehouses to store and sell rice paid to them as land tax by their villagers. In order to protect their booty from wild fluctuations between harvests, they formed the Dojima Rice Market, which was set up in the house of a wealthy rice merchant. There, the merchants gathered, and with shouts and gestures, they negotiated the price of their "rice tickets." Ostensibly, this was the world's first organized futures exchange.

Meanwhile, still others argue that the open outcry for transactions between buyers and sellers preceded the Dojima premises by a number of centuries. Ancient Phoenicians, Greeks, and Romans openly traded options against the cargoes of incoming and outgoing ships—often laden with spices (chapter 2). And in the tenth and twelfth centuries, during seasonal merchant fairs in Brussels, Madrid, and elsewhere, merchants would gather to loudly and openly negotiate for the future delivery of merchandise. Regardless of when or where the world's first true market originated, it was not until 1826 in England, and two decades later in the United States, that the traditional open-outcry futures market was established.

Because this book is about trading in the United States, let's focus on the first U.S. futures mart: the Chicago Board of Trade (CBOT) in 1848. Chicago became the trading hub of the United States, as it represented the great railroad center for moving products grown in the West to the population centers in the East. In 1848, the CBOT opened its doors for trading in grain—specifically, wheat—to become the world's largest futures exchange during most of its history. Its building, erected in 1885 at La Salle Street and Jackson Boulevard, became the symbol of Chicago's commercial vitality.

Just a couple of decades later, in 1860, the New York Produce Exchange opened for business, and within fourteen years, in 1874, the Chicago Produce Exchange (later to become the Chicago Mercantile Exchange [CME]) was formed. The rivalry between the two Chicago exchanges was particularly fierce; the CBOT was painted as the white-glove grain-trading granddaddy of the futures market, while the newer CME was considered a scrappier upstart, a magnet for myriad immigrant groups seeking to make their fortunes through livestock trade.

Over time, the exchanges would splinter into smaller groups and consolidate and sometimes splinter off yet again (figures 1 and 2). We've come a long way from the nineteenth-century patchwork of commodities markets. We no longer trade molasses on the New York Coffee and Sugar Exchange, and we no longer trade eggs on the Chicago Butter and Egg Board. Nearly all the independent marts have consolidated over the decades, now rolling up in the agglomerated CME Group in Chicago and the IntercontinentalExchange in New York. Meanwhile, the West Coast exchanges have long since flickered out altogether (for more on these exchanges, see chapter 4).

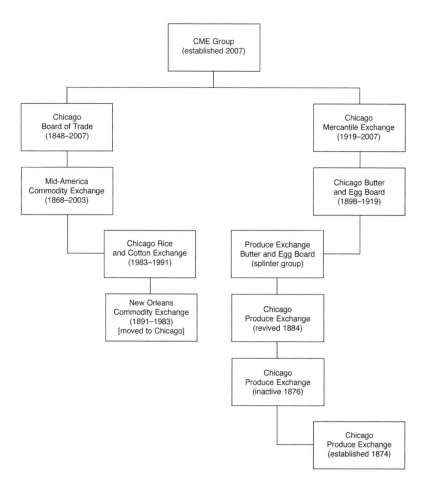

Figure 1 Chicago commodity exchanges.

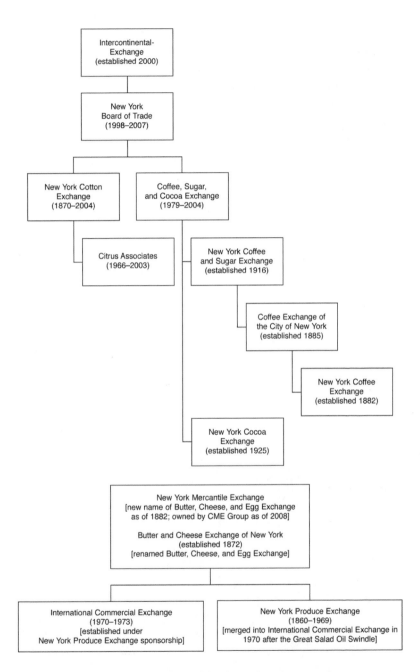

Figure 2 New York commodity exchanges.

This book makes evident that the history of America's commodity exchanges runs a parallel course with the history of industrialization and technology. The mercantile system began as something not far removed from an open-air farmers market, with goods (or the promise of future goods) exchanged for money. But the development of the telegraph enabled traders to sync up prices around the country and around the world, to learn when foodstuffs would be coming to market—not to mention key news about how natural disasters and other events might affect the quantity and quality of those goods. Improvements in canals and later the railroad system, along with the advent of refrigerated rail cars, would help speed the delivery of goods and change the face of the nation—including where the financial markets would centralize. The markets would move to within reach of the farms and livestock slaughterhouses and within reach of the human sprawl mobilizing westward.

With this movement and change, the floors of those financial markets have evolved considerably: gone are the chalkboards and whiteboards on which prices would be feverishly written and erased over and over again. Prices are digitized now. Gone, too, are the once ankle-deep thicket of paper trading tickets; those also have become digitized. The exchange floors, once noted for their teeming throngs of humanity, have thinned somewhat as more trading migrates online and off-exchange. The colorful jackets, hoarse shouting across the pits, and hand signals for communicating orders still exist, but every trader has a smartphone in his or her pocket, and the smartphone buzz is part of the din. The commodities market continues to change and evolve.

How the Modern Commodities Market Works

Although this book is largely dedicated to telling the stories of those long-ago exchanges, it is important to understand the vital role of today's exchanges as well. Hopefully, knowing the history *and* the present will help put each into greater context.

I will leave the deep-dive explanations of the inner workings of the financial markets to the business school professors (and, specifically, to the Institute for Financial Markets, for those seeking reference materials). But to understand the role that the markets play in the food chain, it is important to start with a few key concepts.

- *What is a futures contract?* A futures contract is defined as an agreement between two parties. It commits one to make delivery (sell) on and the other to take delivery (buy) of a stipulated quantity and grade of commodity (or other specified item) at an agreed-upon price on or before a given date in the future. Futures are traded on gold, silver, and oil, as well as on many other nonfood commodities, in addition to "agricultural" or food-based commodities.
- *Who are the key players in the futures markets?* It is easy to think of the commodities market players as belonging to a homogeneous group. But you'll find a few different types in the marketplace — it is one reason it can sometimes be difficult to understand market moves. Each has a different motivation for the decisions it makes. For example:

Risk management. Some buyers and sellers are trying to manage risks and use the futures market to lock in a price for later purchases or sales — for example, a farmer who wants to fix a price at planting time for corn or wheat to be harvested at a future date, or food processors that want to set a price in advance for grain that will be turned into pasta or bread.

Speculation. Meanwhile, others are speculators hoping to make money by correctly guessing how prices will move. These speculators may have no other business connection to the product they are trading and generally have no intention of ever owning corn, wheat, or hogs. Indeed, there are some traders who proudly profess to having never seen in raw form the commodity they trade — that is, fields of soybeans or sugarcane plants. These speculators often are blamed for excess volatility in the markets.

Hedging and passive investment. Still others buy futures contracts as part of an investment strategy or as a hedge against inflation. Because food prices may move in a different direction than stock or bond prices, some investors see the purchase of futures contracts as a way to diversify their portfolios. Again, many investors in this category have never seen the commodities and have never set foot on a trading floor. Further, just as many owners of mutual funds don't know which companies they hold in their stock portfolios, many investors don't know which commodities contracts are included in their index funds.

• *What drives commodity prices?* It is important to note the wide range of influences considered in trading futures contracts.

Some market participants focus on market fundamentals—factors affecting current and future supply and demand for a product. For food-based contracts, this may include the weather, the state of the economy, exchange rates, fuel prices, and all the other factors that influence supply and demand for a product.

However, other traders focus less on these fundamentals and rely on other techniques to predict how prices are likely to change, such as in technical trading, which relies on charts of historical prices to discern future patterns. Others use statistical techniques to predict price movements.

Further, those investing in commodities as a way to balance a portfolio or hedge against inflation pay little attention to day-to-day developments in futures markets.

• *What's the difference between food and "food commodities"?* In some cases, there's not much difference (e.g., arabica versus robusta coffee; grade AA versus grade AAA butter), but often, the difference is quite stark. All commodities are assigned a grade, so a standard is imposed on what is bought and sold. But that grade is often below what most consumers would choose to purchase. Corn is probably the most striking example—grain market specialist Chad Hart of Iowa State University refers to "food grade" versus "feed grade."[1] The former is sold as canned corn or ground into corn flakes; the latter is used to feed livestock and is distilled into ethanol.

In *The Omnivore's Dilemma*, writer and activist Michael Pollan describes food commodities as "an economic abstraction," as invented in Chicago in the 1950s.[2] For example, instead of buying or selling a particular bushel of corn, traders buy or sell a bushel of corn that meets certain grading standards. Those standards might specify some combination of size, moisture content, level of insect or other damage exhibited, color, or origin. But within those standards, commodities are "without qualities; quantity is the only thing that matters."[3] In other words, commodities contracts aren't about trading the tastiest corn but about enabling the buying and selling of exact amounts of corn that meet these specific standards. Although Pollan's (admittedly justified) complaint is that this system severs the link between the producer of a foodstuff and its ultimate consumer, it makes it far easier to trade, particularly in the large quantities involved in futures trades. One corn futures contract, for example, represents 5,000 bushels (about 127 metric tons) of corn.

How Does the Trading of Commodities Influence *What We Eat* and *What We Pay* for Food?

To help answer this key question, I turned to several economists and financial experts.

- *It helps keep price swings in check.* Without the "effective risk management tool" that hedging provides, explains Alan Bush, senior financial futures analyst with Archer Financial Services, we might be paying quite a bit more at the checkout counter, and price swings would be considerably wider.[4] For example, it is possible for coffee futures to surge 30 percent in a two-week span, but when we pick up a bag of coffee beans at the store, we don't find that the price tag shows an equivalent 30 percent spike; it is likely the same price as the last bag we purchased. "Hedging has the impact of reducing end-user costs," Bush says. "By making markets more efficient and reducing market risk, this allows buyers and producers to effectively know what their price parameters will be within a certain range."[5] Although the commodities market mitigates day-to-day price swings, it doesn't eliminate them altogether. But most experts I spoke with said that the correlation is delayed: assuming the price changes are sustained, higher (or lower) prices on the trading floor generally are not reflected at grocery stores for about a year to a year and a half.
- *It guides manufacturers in establishing food prices.* Some experts, like Bill G. Lapp, president of Advanced Economic Solutions, posit that commodities trading reflects raw material price changes, rather than affecting price changes at the consumer level. He points to a recent release of the U.S. Department of Agriculture (USDA) crop report, which included the government's prediction for the U.S. corn yield and thus caused a change in price for corn futures. "It's not the commodities trading that changes the price," Lapp says. "It's the value of it." The key role that commodities markets play, he adds, is "price discovery"—a term widely used by traders and food manufacturers alike. Essentially, "price discovery" is the process of figuring out how much one can charge for an item, and the prices

quoted in commodities trading provide a handy guide for discovering the price the market will bear. Lapp likens the commodities market to the real estate market: "If there were never any prices revealed in housing transactions, how would you know how much a home is worth? You'd have no comparisons, values per square foot, any sense of how prices are increasing."[6] The communal nature of trading and the public and widespread dissemination of price quotes are equally important. "Otherwise, it would be a much smaller group of people involved in the process of determining the value of a bushel of corn," Lapp warns.[7]

• *It helps restaurants and manufacturers manage costs and profits.* Lapp has a particularly unique viewpoint on the impact of commodities; he works with restaurant companies and food manufacturers to help them manage food costs and risks via the commodities market. The consequences of a 25 percent spike in cattle futures could be calamitous for a large hamburger chain. An increase in menu prices could mean a loss of customers and market share for a significant period—but absorbing the cost could mean an enormous hit to profit margins, potentially affecting earnings for the quarter. "Their profit margins are directly impacted by the swings in the commodities market," Lapp explains. His role is to track input costs for a restaurant and give a prognosis as to where costs may be headed in the next couple of years. "I advise them on whether these are short-term blips or not. For example, if cheese prices are headed higher, will we get some relief in the next months, or will that be a sustained increase? If they take prices up, others will follow. It's an extremely competitive environment. If they make mistakes, it can be a problem that can put them out of business."[8] Some restaurant chains will make substitutions in food products—such as corn syrup for sugar or soybean oil for corn oil—or will even change entire restaurant concepts based on anticipated prices for commodities.

Clearly, commodities prices influence what we eat when we go out to restaurants as well as what we pay at the supermarket. Sometimes, they also affect what gets planted in the first place. Chad Hart explains how farmers use commodities prices to make decisions: "As a farmer, I can decide whether to plant soybeans or corn. Which will provide a better price for me at harvest? Or I can decide the amount to grow. Futures provide a signal. Is it necessarily an accurate signal? No. But it's the best signal we have. People are actually willing to put up contracts and make trades. It represents an actual transaction that will occur."[9]

• *The impact of commodities trading changes over time.* It is also important to understand how commodities trading has evolved. Hart estimates that for every dollar spent on food, 15 to 20 cents represents the raw commodities used in that product. The rest represents advertising, transportation and fuel, labor, real estate, and other inputs. He also points to a 2008 study by the USDA, which figured out how much went into creating a box of corn flakes. "They figured out you paid more for the packaging surrounding those flakes than you did for the corn in the corn flakes!" he crows. "What this tells you is that while food prices can move dramatically, in the scheme of things, they are not a big part of what goes into the price of those corn flakes."[10]

Now, this is a discouraging concept for someone who is researching the connection between commodities and food. But Hart quickly reassures that, historically, the connection was much tighter, and that it is important to understand how the role has changed over time: "If you go back to the 1940s and 1950s, I'd argue that commodities had a greater influence. There was less packaging and food didn't travel as far—there were fewer inputs than the agricultural costs that went into food. Over time, we have seen an erosion in [commodities'] impact on food prices," and commodities swings have exerted less and less influence.[11]

However, there is one notable exception. "The organic, local food, and community garden movements bring back the idea that the main cost we would like to see in our food is the agricultural product underneath," Hart explains, and the excitement in his voice is audible. "As we look at those food systems, we bring back the percentage that is related to the underlying commodity."[12] Just as the utility of commodities trading has evolved from early iterations in Japan and Holland, it continues to evolve with every product we buy and sell today, whether through an organized exchange or a community farmers market.

This is an inspiring concept indeed.

The New York Produce Exchange (1899), where black pepper futures traded from 1937 to 1957, when the building was demolished. (Library of Congress, Prints and Photographs Division)

CHAPTER TWO

The Spice Route

History showed that the pepper market
can be as fiery as the condiment itself.
NEW YORK TIMES, JUNE 13, 1937

Spices were dubbed "gray gold." Peppercorns were known as "black gold." Throughout history, spices have been firmly linked with currency and commerce, arguably more so than any other foodstuff. Spices—specifically peppercorns—were traded for several decades in the United States commodity markets and continue to trade actively in India today.

Without spices, we might not have a financial marketplace in the United States because the pursuit of pungent spices led to the "discovery" of America. Even the derivation of the word "spice" points toward value and currency. It is linked to the Latin noun *species*, from which the English language derives a whole family of words, including "special," "specification," "species," and "especially." Originally, the Latin word meant simply "type" or "kind," a definition that survives in English as the word "specie," as reserved for cash "in kind"—that is, "coinage." In Roman usage, *species* quite often implied value, and in time, it acquired an even more specific meaning. The word came to be used to denote the "type" or "kind" of article on which import duty was payable; and it seems to have been in this context that it gave rise to the French term *épicé* (related to *épicerie* [grocery], another food/commerce connection) and the English word "spice."[1]

Why was such value assigned to spices, particularly in the Old World? Although the answer is complicated (and entire books have been devoted to this subject), one answer is that spices were valued because they were extremely difficult to obtain. Historians point to a number of early uses for spices — for adding flavor and piquancy to food, of course. But they were also considered to hold medicinal and mystical properties. In the Middle East and Europe, spices were treated as basic ingredients in incense, embalming preservatives, ointments, perfumes, antidotes against poisons, cosmetics, and medicines; they were used only to a limited extent in the kitchen. Hippocrates (460–377 B.C.E.), also known as the father of medicine, was among those who mentioned spices in his writing.

Spices were first used in Rome in the first century C.E. The Romans were not the first Europeans to eat pepper, but they were the first to do so with any regularity.[2] Further, the Romans were the most extravagant users of aromatics in history. Spices were employed lavishly in the kitchen, cosmetics, and elsewhere. Spice-flavored wines were in demand because spices were supposed to add "heat" to the banquet. Indeed, a recipe for spiced wine appears in Marcus Gavius Apicius's book, *De re coquinaria* (*On the Subject of Cooking*), the only surviving cookbook from antiquity — specifically, from the first century C.E.[3] The famous Roman gourmand spiked his "Fine Spiced Wine," a "Honey Refresher for Travelers," with saffron and crushed pepper (some translators suggest the intended spice was beads of allspice, rather than peppercorns, even though allspice came from the New World). It's worth noting that pepper appears in 349 of the book's 468 recipes.[4] Too much eating at the banquet? No problem. Apicius also created a recipe for "Spiced Salts," to ward against indigestion. He mixes salt with white pepper, ginger, celery seed, and thyme seed.[5] And after such a feast, many Romans would sleep it off on costly saffron-filled pillows, believing they would avoid a hangover.[6] The one thing spices could not do was preserve foods. Salt and sugar (neither is classified as a spice) are key food preservatives. Whereas spices add flavor and piquancy, and might stimulate the appetite, they are unable to assist in the important utilitarian task of halting food spoilage. On a related note, although it has long been suggested that spices were used historically to disguise the flavor of rotten meat, making it more palatable, modern culinary historians have debunked this myth.

What was the real value of spices in Roman times? Prestige. Exotic fragrances and flavors announced themselves as luxuries and advertised a consumer's extravagance. "The prestige function of spices can scarcely be exaggerated," John Keay writes. "Like fine silks and acknowledged works of art, exotic fragrances and flavours lent to aspiring households an air of superior refinement and enviable opulence. They conferred distinction."[7]

Commodity exchanges as we know them today have their roots in this time period. The fairs and marketplaces that sprang up in the Middle Ages were the descendants of the Greek markets (*agorai*) and the markets of Rome (*fora vendalia*), which specialized in distributing specific commodities (spices included). Although almost all the trading at these fairs was for merchandise immediately available ("spot" sales), at times, contracts were drawn up to sell merchandise "to arrive" or "for delivery" at some future time. These contracts made up the crude beginnings of what is now called a futures market.

During the Dark Ages, which followed the fall of the Roman Empire, there was little international trade, and commerce generally was confined to small areas. The feudal system dominated the countryside. Only in the walled cities were people free to retain and develop the specialized knowledge necessary for efficient production and distribution of goods and services. As medieval fairs—where goods could be displayed and traded—declined, first market centers sprang up and later the bourses and exchanges. Initially, these were operated in public squares on the town common; they dealt in all types of commodities. As political stability improved, so did economic conditions. Specialization in markets dealing in certain commodities came about—although they would not crystallize in the form we know today until many centuries later.

Middle Ages and Spices

Spices were still highly valued during the Middle Ages—long after the fall of the Roman Empire. In fact, peppercorns, cinnamon, and ginger were used as currency to pay taxes, tolls, rents, and dowries. Pepper was the most ubiquitous spice, and the one most often used in place of currency.

So important were spices, they famously launched Christopher Columbus around the world, as he searched for a route to the Indies on behalf of the Spanish monarchy. And most important for Americans, this spice lust led to the discovery of the New World—without which the following chapters about markets in New York and Chicago would be nonexistent. According to Henry Hobhouse: "The starting point for the European expansion out of the Mediterranean and the Atlantic continental shelf had nothing to do with, say, religion or the rise of capitalism—but it had a great deal to do with pepper. The Americas were discovered as a byproduct in the search for pepper."[8] Although Columbus famously found the route to the New World instead of a route to the Indies, he also found spices. "I believe I have found rhubarb and cinnamon," Columbus had reported after his first voyage. However, Columbus found the "wrong" spices—not cinnamon, peppercorns, and other Indian spices, but instead fiery capsicum (chile) peppers, allspice berries, and vanilla, the last of which would change the face of European confectionary. In the decades that followed, the Spanish, as well as the Portuguese, gradually established their hold on spice trading.

Meanwhile, for the other parts of Europe more estranged from the bulk spice trade, spices played a different role in mercantile life. Pepper first appeared in the economic life of England in the eleventh century, as ships arriving in London at Christmas or Easter were commanded to produce 10 pounds of pepper in part payment of a tax. By 1180, London's "pepperers" had created a guild, called the Pepperers' Company, that would emerge as one of the city's earliest livery entities.[9] In the fifteenth century, the Pepperers' Company renamed itself the Grossers' to reflect both the city's growing trade in spices and the Grossers' role in their "grossing," or wholesaling. In England, "grossery" then diversified into related commodities, like sugar, and from there into general provisioning. It also opted for the alternative spelling of "grocery." A similar development occurred in France, although there the grocers retained their original designation as spicers—*épiciers*—hence, the still-familiar *épicerie*.[10]

Because it was so heavily traded, pepper eventually lost its "golden" status and fell to be considered among the most prosaic of spices. To meet growing demand in Europe during the late sixteenth and very early seventeenth centuries, pepper became overcultivated and difficult to regulate.

"Cultivation was being extended up the Malabar coast towards Goa, across the water to Sri Lanka and Malaya, and throughout the interior regions of Sumatra and western Java. No nation could hope to police so many outlets," Keay describes. Eventually, the market became flooded. "*Piper negrum* had ceased to conform to the enticing commercial profile of a spice and became just another bulk commodity. Pepper 'mountains' accumulated in the warehouses of the European companies. In the last years of Cromwellian London, the price slumped to as little as 7*d*. a pound. In Amsterdam pepper was occasionally sold at a loss."[11] Meanwhile, some markets coped by focusing instead on the higher-value "fine spices."

Although European explorers, particularly the Dutch and Portuguese, would continue to search for new spice islands and spice routes to control the lucrative flow of the spice trade, by the nineteenth century, spices were no longer viewed as exotic. "Pepper-pot" stews were considered mundane affairs for the middle and lower classes and not to be eaten by courtiers.[12]

Futures Markets

Interestingly, just as the heyday of the spice trade was ending, the fledgling United States entered the spice fray at the end of the eighteenth century, importing Sumatran pepper to Salem, Massachusetts. Although the United States has never been a driving force in the spice trade as it has in trading corn, coffee, or cattle, the New York marts traded pepper, at least for a brief and spotty interlude, from the 1930s through the 1960s.

On June 16, 1937, the New York Produce Exchange began trading in black pepper futures, joining cottonseed oil, tallow, and frozen egg contracts: "The black pepper contract called for 33,000 pounds of Lampong pepper, with Aleppy [Aleppo] and Tellicherry as optional deliveries. Over-the-counter trading in black pepper futures had been conducted for several months prior to beginning official trade."[13] At first, the reporting of this event was jubilant. Prior to the New York contract, London's spice merchants in Mincing Lane had taken the primary role in setting pepper prices. Just days before trading commenced, the *New York Times* reported, "Optimistic brokers predict that New York will henceforth assume first place in the pepper trade, basing their enthusiasm on the fact that the United States consumes more than 30 per cent of the world's production of pepper and that current stocks in this country are twice as large as those held in England."

Further, "History showed that the pepper market can be as fiery as the condiment itself. A year ago or so the Mincing Lane spice brokers promoted a boom in pepper which collapsed when the 1936 crop proved to be the largest in history; spices dropped to the lowest level since the turn of the century. It may be that New York will provide the stabilizing influence that the pepper market has long needed. Just now, the chastened Mincing Lane brokers are content with their nutmegs, mace and caraway seed."[14] However, New York's efforts in trading pepper contracts proved modest at best. A total of fifty-nine contracts changed hands on the first day of trading—a slow start—but gathered momentum in the following weeks, with predecessors of Merrill Lynch, Lehman Brothers, Prudential, and JPMorgan Chase joining the fray in the black pepper market.[15]

As with a great many other financial concerns, the advent of World War II shut down trading in black pepper futures from July 1 through December 2, 1946. Although wartime rationing meant severe limitations on which foodstuffs could be obtained, the impact on the use of pepper in American cooking was minimal, and most recipes from this time continued to call for black pepper as seasoning. When trading was reopened, the *Wall Street Journal* reported, hopefully: "Pepper is reaching the United States in increased volume. It was estimated that at least 5,000 tons of black pepper will arrive from the Far East some time this month. Shipment[s] thus far since the end of the war have been negligible." Despite this, "annual world production of pepper before the war amounted to about 65,000 tons. Of this total, the United States normally consumed about 15,000 tons."[16]

However, this effort proved less robust than before the war, and soon trading was halted again. It did not resume until April 1960, with each contract revised to represent 10 tons of Lampong black or Malabar garbled black pepper.[17] By this time, the New York Produce Exchange contract was the sole black pepper futures market in the Western Hemisphere; the only other place black pepper futures traded was in Cochin (today, Kochi), on the southwestern coast of India. As usual, where there was money to be made, it didn't take long for wrongdoing to escalate. "Black Pepper Prices Soar Under Squeeze," proclaimed a *New York Times* headline. "Americans are going to find that much of the spice in their lives has grown more costly," the article read. "Pepper, the kind most savor[ed], is going up in price. After more than four years of stability, the wholesale quotation for pepper has begun to climb as demand outpaces supply." Wholesale prices for black pepper—the most widely used spice in the country both then and now—had soared more than 200 percent during the previous seven months.[18]

The upsurge was attributed to lower worldwide pepper production and greater global consumption, as well as to charges that sizable pepper supplies were being held by a few large interests. One market expert speculated that shipments were going to "Communist countries" at the expense of U.S. spice lovers. The same *New York Times* article attributed the cornering of the market to a Singapore syndicate, the Wan Tong Trading Company, which in 1958 began secretly buying up large amounts of pepper: "Some of the supplies the syndicate bought were dumped back on the market to keep supplies moving and to induce other traders to keep selling. By the end of 1959, the company's plan began to show results. It had obtained a sizable share of the available pepper, forcing prices to climb from 40 cents a pound last November to about 85 cents in January."[19]

Here, the pepper futures trail goes cold; no references to black pepper futures exist after the early 1960s. Even representatives of the IntercontinentalExchange, which supersedes the Produce Exchange, had no idea when peppercorn futures might have ceased trading. The final reference found is December 9, 1963, which notes that the principal business of the Produce Exchange had become cottonseed oil futures, "although a few contracts of black pepper are traded from time to time."[20]

It is somewhat mysterious that black pepper was the only spice determined to be tradable in the United States. Even as commodities markets set pricing for pepper, the U.S. government still tracked imports and pricing, at least monthly, on a wide array of spices, including white pepper, cayenne pepper, cinnamon, cassia, nutmeg, clove, and vanilla beans, as well as seeds including anise, caraway, cardamom, coriander, fennel, mustard, and poppy.[21] The Foreign Agricultural Service division of the USDA still disseminates "New York Spot Prices" for a wide array of spices. This includes the pepper the United States obtains from its three largest suppliers: Indonesia (Lampong black, Muntok white) is the top exporter to the United States, India (Malabar black, Tellicherry) is second, and Brazil (Brazilian black) is third. Of all the spices, black pepper alone accounts for nearly 35 percent of the world's spice trade.[22]

India's Spice Markets

The bulk of futures trading in spices, including pepper, now takes place in India. The oldest pepper exchange is run by the India Pepper and Spice Trade Association (IPSTA). It is located in the port city of Kochi, which is the financial capital of the state of Kerala, on India's southwestern Malabar Coast. The location is no accident. In the sixteenth and seventeenth centuries, when the Portuguese (and later the Dutch) colonized India, pepper vines were cultivated in the mountains, and the dried berries were brought down to the port for shipping.

The IPSTA began futures trading in pepper in September 1957 and focused specifically on that single commodity. Though by most accounts the trading floor is now deserted, it once bustled with activity; as recently as 2003, a visiting reporter described the scene in this way: "40 or so brokers in pepper futures—some in Western sports shirts, others in white Indian loincloths called dhotis, all in bare feet to protect the polished floor—put up a hellish if episodic din. Between napping and gesturing like a company of Barrymores, they shout and curse into their telephones." Many of the traders acted for brokers for large firms, including American companies, such as spice purveyor McCormick & Company. Meanwhile, outside the air-conditioned buildings, "just enough warehouses remain on the congested streets to perfume the warm air with a gingery-peppery clove-and-cardamom amalgam of aromas."[23]

Today, although pepper continues to trade hands at a brisk pace, the exchange building has become a tourist attraction, and trading is computerized, with traders located either at off-exchange offices or at home.[24] In addition to Kochi, the National Commodity & Derivatives Exchange (NCDEX) also trades pepper. Malabar garbled pepper—the same Malabar peppercorns carried down the mountains of Kerala in the seventeenth century—today accounts for nearly 90 percent of the total spice exports from India[25] and is the standard for modern pepper trading. While pepper remains "the king of spices," fragrant cardamom, "the queen of spices," is traded on the Multi Commodity Exchange (MCX) as well as on the National Multi Commodity Exchange (NMCE), both spices trading in 100 kilogram units. Meanwhile, in addition to pepper, the NCDEX trades turmeric (which also appears on the NMCE), jeera (better known to

Westerners as cumin), chile (bright red capsicum peppers), and coriander (also traded on the MCX).[26]

From a global culinary and trade perspective, black pepper consistently ranks among the leading spices used by virtually every culture. No wonder it has been valued as "gray gold" and the "king of spices." Certainly, pepper has retained its position as a highly tradable and valued commodity in the global marketplace—and the undisputed king of the spice rack.

Corn: The Food of the Nation (World War I poster, 1918). (Library of Congress, Prints and Photographs Division)

CHAPTER THREE

The Commodity That Built a Nation

Corn Futures

Buy Corn and Wear Diamonds
NEW YORK TIMES, AUGUST 13, 1897

Indigenous Americans introduced the world to corn. We have embraced it in cooking and never looked back. Corn has had an enormous impact on both America's foodways and its economy. As Michael Pollan neatly demonstrates in *The Omnivore's Dilemma*, corn is ubiquitous in our diets. It is the largest crop in the United States, both in terms of the value of the crop and the acres planted. In addition to its use in myriad processed and nonprocessed foods, as animal feed, and as a by-product for nonedible items from gasoline to adhesives, corn is seemingly everywhere.[1] Speculators have aimed to profit from corn's ubiquity, trading not only corn futures but, at one point, high-fructose corn syrup futures too.

It is no wonder, then, that corn trades so ferociously today. Trading volume in corn futures regularly trumps any other food-based commodity trading in the United States, and in 2010, corn prices skyrocketed 45 percent, second only to coffee in terms of price inflation.[2] And although the Chicago Board of Trade (CBOT) is the largest futures market for corn and we "corn-fed" Americans are legendary consumers of the "yellow grain," plenty of other commodities marts trade corn too: the Bolsa de Mercadorias & Futuros in Brazil, the Budapest Commodity Exchange in Hungary, the Kanmon Commodity Exchange in Korea, the Marché à Terme

International de France, the Mercado a Término de Buenos Aires in Argentina, and the Tokyo Grain Exchange.

Like so many other staple foods in early America, corn had a dual identity as food and commodity. Indeed, this dual identity made corn indispensable to the slave trade: corn was both the currency traders used to pay for slaves in Africa and the food upon which slaves subsisted during their passage to America.[3]

The Geography of Corn

Corn is indigenous to the Americas. Although it has made its way to every other continent in the world, it has its origins here, and it seems fitting that the agricultural power of the United States, in the words of historian Arturo Warman, "rests firmly on a solid foundation of corn."[4] Explorers brought corn back to their Asian and European countries as a novelty, but it first took root outside the Americas in post-Columbian Europe. Corn flourished in the warmer climates, and in the mid-sixteenth century, corn cultivation started in Spain and Portugal, soon extending into neighboring France. A second early nucleus flourished along the Mediterranean (such as Italy, where corn was ground into polenta in Venice and other north-central regions) and eventually spread throughout the valleys of the alpine piedmont until it reached Austria and the Balkans. By the eighteenth century, corn figured as a common crop in the southern half of France. On the eve of the nineteenth century, it had a firm hold in European agriculture and was found everywhere, consumed as corn flour primarily in two ways: it was mixed with other flours to produce low-quality breads and it was cooked in water to form a paste.[5] (Interestingly, in the cooler northern climates, another vegetable from the Americas took hold as a food staple: the potato, which has Andean origins. Both the potato and corn came to bear the stigma of food for the poor, and in the end, while the potato blight ravaged Ireland's potato crops and brought famine to the Irish, much of the poor in corn-fed southern Europe fell prey to pellagra, an oft-fatal niacin deficiency related to excessive corn consumption.)[6]

As America pushed its frontiers westward, slowly deforesting land and planting the fields that would soon yield massive corn exports back across the Atlantic, Europe cultivated its own corn fields. Corn's high yield was one of the most frequently cited reasons for its introduction throughout Europe. Conventional wisdom placed the average yield for corn prior to the nineteenth century at between two and three times that of traditional Old World cereals.[7] However, it had another advantage: corn used land that ordinarily lay fallow during the summer and made it productive. "The traditional European staple cereals—wheat, rye, barley and oats— were winter or spring crops," Warman explains. "Corn did not compete with them so much as complement them."[8] At the beginning of the nineteenth century, Warman estimates, corn already had an impact on at least 40 percent of Europe's population, meaning that people both produced and ate corn or ate other things that had been grown in association with corn. "Corn was integral to the dietary system," he concludes. "Corn's role loomed large as the nineteenth century progressed. Diets changed the most radically as population growth reached its most accelerated pace to date. Growing urbanization spurred the separation of producers and consumers. . . . European growth relied on American plants."[9]

Corn Exchanges

One of the earliest organized exchanges was London's Mark Lane Corn Exchange, which started operating in 1746. At this time, "corn" was a generic English word for any kind of grain, even a grain of salt (hence the term "corned beef"), long before maize ("Indian corn") was known in Europe. The German word *korn* means "grain."[10]

By the time the Corn Exchange was established in New York in 1840, "corn" clearly meant "maize" to American traders, even though it was referred to as "yellow grain" in headlines for decades following. Both corn and grain were traded at the Corn Exchange and the CBOT, also established in the 1840s, and in early newspaper accounts, the two words are often used interchangeably. By the 1860s, traders began to deal in contracts that met a specific description (e.g., a certain grade of corn), which makes it easier for modern-day researchers to track the trajectory of individual commodities.

The New York Corn Exchange's trading scene is described in an 1861 article from the *Working Farmer*: "The provision dealers form one extreme portion of the crowd; the dealers in grain the centre, and the dealers in

CORN WHISKEY

Another form of concentrated corn—alcoholic beverages—has played a key part in early America. Distillation reduced the sheer volume of corn and created yet another commodity product for trade, while also providing for home consumption. The earliest colonists consumed beer made with fermented blue or black corn, and distilled corn liquor soon followed. Captain George Thorpe, a gentleman pensioner and a Cambridge University scholar known for his "godliness and learning," fired up a still on the banks of the James River in Virginia and produced authentic corn liquor—what we would now regard as moonshine. The captain wrote to London, circa 1620: "I have found a way to make so good a drink of Indian corn as I protest I have divers [sic] times refused to drink good strong English beer and chosen to drink that." Although surely not everyone found early corn whiskey as delightfully ambrosial, another batch of Virginia corn whiskey found its way across the Potomac to Washington, where its recipient, Gene Fowler, said the liquid "tasted as though it had been keeping company with old 'tater sacks.'"* The corn-based Kentucky whiskey specifically known as bourbon, which blends both corn and grain distillates, is said to have originated in the late eighteenth century and is named for Bourbon County, although there's some dispute as to precisely where and when it was first produced. The term "bourbon" didn't become common until after the Civil War.†

During the colonial period, rum was the preferred tipple, and by comparison, whiskey was considered "a more rustic beverage." However, whiskey

flour the other extreme. The flour dealers are examining samples in small green boxes, or mixing small quantities of flour with water, and testing the strength and color of the dough. The grain dealers are handling and chewing and scattering wheat and corn upon the floor from small cotton bags taken from the pocket; and the provision dealers, having no samples, do their business by unassisted conversation."[11]

Little by little, corn developed more importance in culinary and mercantile life. For example, a bold, if premature, statement printed on a Civil War envelope declared, "Corn (Not cotton.) is King."[12] In 1889, Colonel Charles Murphy of the New York Corn Exchange developed a special *Corn Show* at the Paris Exposition with the support of the U.S. Department of was the preferred alcoholic beverage among the frontier pioneers, "who did not buy anything they did not directly produce themselves." The many merchants who traded with Native Americans and fur trappers preferred corn whiskey as well.[‡]

Taxation played a key role in corn whiskey's popularity. In 1794, when the federal government tried to impose an excise tax on whiskey, a rebellion broke out that required the mobilization of fifteen thousand militiamen to contain it. The struggle between tax collectors and bootleggers did not end until well into the twentieth century. Large rum distilleries could not bear this tax burden on top of certain changes in international trade, further contributing to the immense popularity of corn liquor in the nineteenth century. Between 1790 and 1820, when consumption was at its peak, Americans drank an average of slightly more than 5 gallons of whiskey a year. Corn was converted to whiskey at the rate of six to one, or a bushel of corn per gallon of whiskey—a conversion rate that was very similar to that of corn to pig; 5 pounds of corn supposedly equaled 1 pound of weight "on the hoof."[§]

*Quoted in Gerald Carson, *The Social History of Bourbon* (Lexington: University Press of Kentucky, 2010), 30.

†Ibid., 43.

‡Arturo Warman, *Corn and Capitalism: How a Botanical Bastard Grew to Global Dominance* (Chapel Hill: University of North Carolina Press, 2003), 176.

§Ibid., 177.

Agriculture, "to demonstrate to the Old World visitors the value of Indian corn as a material for human food," complete with an "American kitchen" for preparing foods made with corn.[13] But it was a slow build. Even as the Corn Exchange evolved into the New York Produce Exchange, the East Coast center for corn trade, and the CBOT flourished in the Midwest, also trading corn, the yellow grain lacked the trading cachet of wheat for much of the nineteenth century.

Compared with wheat or cotton—both high-profile and widely considered cash crops—corn's impact was more subtle. In contrast to the relatively more localized midwestern sea of wheat and southern cotton plantations, corn grew everywhere and yielded more, which tended to devalue its worth.

Even during the height of the pre–Civil War cotton boom years, corn occupied between five and twelve times the total surface area planted in cotton among the fifteen slave states. However, the value of corn was two-thirds that of cotton. Warman refers to corn as "the clandestine king," compared with the lauded "King Cotton." "Unlike cotton, corn was everywhere," he says. "It was sown on the smallest farms in the poorest districts as well as on large cotton and tobacco plantations. While virtually all the cotton was sold for cash on the commercial market, providing the engine for mercantile consumption and profit, a very considerable part of the corn crop never left the unit where it was produced," often used for food or as animal feed—or processed into beer or whiskey.[14] The disparity was clear: cotton was for the rich and powerful; corn was for the poor. Corn was the main staple of slave diets (the standard ration of corn for slaves was a peck of corn a week, or about 2 pounds of corn a day).[15] After the Civil War disrupted the southern economy, production was significantly restructured, and food crops trumped cotton crops. Corn assumed greater value in day-to-day production, as well as in the southern diet, but it would be many decades before it would be so valued in the trading pits.

The Corn–Pig Cycle

As with much of America's commerce, westward expansion and mass transportation, including the evolution of domestic rail, river transport systems, and conveyance by sea, played pivotal roles in turning corn into a valued and tradable product. During the late nineteenth century in particular, corn moved from mere crop to full-fledged commodity. And much of corn's value revolved around its potential for feeding livestock.

Corn did not play an important role in North America's early foreign trade. Corn already had been cultivated throughout Europe, and it grew well in many areas there. However, the colder winters and hotter summers of the New World meant a wider repertoire of products could be grown, particularly on the southern plantations, and used for trade. Tobacco was the first chief export product during the colonial era, followed by cotton. But corn was not exported back to Europe. It was grown on the northern farms and the southern plantations. Corn was consumed domestically by families, by the workforce, and most important, by livestock. Even if

Americans didn't enjoy eating corn (wheat was the preferred foodstuff), livestock certainly did.

Swine and large livestock traditionally were fattened up, or "finished," with corn before going to the slaughterhouse, or before walking the long road to central areas, like Cincinnati (or "Porkopolis") or the cattle center of Abilene, Kansas, where they would be inspected, traded, and eventually slaughtered. Indeed, swine and cattle were thought of as concentrated corn. "The hog," wrote one British journalist in 1887, "is regarded as the most compact form in which the Indian corn crop of the States can be transported to market. Hence the corn is fed to the hog on the farm, and he is sent to Chicago as a package provided by nature for its utilization."[16] Quipped another nineteenth-century commenter, "The hog eats the corn, and Europe eats the Hog. Corn thus becomes incarnate; for what is a hog, but fifteen or twenty bushels of corn on four legs?"[17] An empirical rule of thumb dictated that 5 pounds of corn was necessary for a pig to gain 1 pound of weight on the hoof. This rule allowed producers, upon comparing prices, to make decisions about whether to raise pigs as opposed to selling corn—what became known as the "corn–pig cycle." Another, less savory rule of thumb was that four cows fed with corn generated enough waste to raise one pig; however, it was rarely mentioned that the "waste" was in the form of cattle excrement.[18] Thanks to the advent of refrigerated transportation compartments, corn-fed U.S. livestock was exported to Europe at ever-increasing rates. According to one estimate, by the nineteenth century, America was responsible for 90 percent of England's beef imports (for more on this, see chapter 7). Another estimate calculates that for the decade between 1890 and 1900, the corn grown for all purposes and the meat produced by livestock fed on corn had a combined value that was greater than the value of all other agricultural products put together.[19]

The relationship was symbiotic, if not downright circular. As export demand for American livestock increased, more corn was grown to feed the animals; as more corn was available, a greater share was apportioned for feeding livestock. In the nineteenth century, the Midwest became home to a well-defined corn belt, making up what today are the states of Iowa, Illinois—the two corn giants—Nebraska, Minnesota, Wisconsin, Indiana, Michigan, and Ohio. Those fertile lands produced yields of 40 to 60 bushels per acre—1.1 to 1.7 tons per acre—which were twice the U.S. average at the time. In coming years, corn production would spread beyond the

WILL CORN-PRICE SHIFTS SPELL THE END OF GRASS-FED BEEF?

If you would like to taste food history—literally—in the form of grass-fed beef, either find yourself a small rancher in the United States who insists on feeding cattle primarily on grasses or head down to Argentina. But if the latter is what you have in mind, you'd best book that plane ticket posthaste.

Until recently, Argentina was known for its superior beef, which was attributed to a diet of grasses rather than grains. The flavor used to be a selling point for Argentina, which had a long, proud history as the world's greatest exporter of beef, supplied from cows that grazed on the endless pampas under the gauchos' watchful eyes (the Argentinean version of cattle raised on the vast prairies by cowboys). According to those who have sampled both grass-fed and grain-fed beef, the former is reportedly chewier but cleaner tasting and less fatty; longer aging times are often used to tenderize the meat. Also, grass feed is better for the animals and more sustainable for the environment, advocates say. Some assert that grass-fed beef is better for human consumers too.

corn belt. The far-flung region known loosely as "corn country" soon included South Dakota, Oklahoma, Missouri, Kansas, Kentucky, and Tennessee. Texas, notably, a prime cattle state, became one of the ten largest corn-producing states. "Corn," says Warman, "was probably the only crop cultivated in every state of the Union."[20]

But if it's possible to pinpoint when corn truly becomes a commodity, that would be around 1910, when the United States produced a little more than 2.5 trillion bushels of corn, almost 70 million tons. This amounted to more than 1,500 pounds for each of the almost 92 million Americans recorded in the 1910 census. In other words, this tremendous volume easily surpassed any demand for corn as food. During this time, more than half and perhaps as much as 80 percent of corn production was destined for cattle, swine, and poultry feed troughs. Certainly, corn had been used previously as animal feed. But never prior to this period had the largest share of corn been used for feed. (This also contrasts starkly with the situation elsewhere. In Mexico, corn accounted for more than two-thirds of

But it has become harder to obtain, thanks to shifting commodity prices. Today, most cattle in Argentina are raised on feedlots, as they are in the United States. This transition has been driven by soaring prices in the global grain market over the past decade, making it far more profitable to grow soybeans, wheat, and corn than herd cattle.

Some chefs have expressed dismay over the shift. "When I first came to Argentina, I said, 'This is what beef is supposed to taste like!' Now, it's just steak," says Dan Perlman, an American chef and writer living in Buenos Aires.*

There's still hope. Those who hanker for grass-fed beef can look to neighboring Uruguay. While the beef industry there is focused on getting international certification for its grass-fed cattle, it's likely that Uruguay's "grass-certified beef" will simply be exported to high-end markets in Europe. On a more local scale, many regions now have smaller beef producers that graze cattle mostly or entirely in grassy pastures—another example of consumers getting closer to agricultural products.

*Quoted in Nancy Shute, "Farewell to Argentina's Famed Beef," National Public Radio, December 8, 2011.

Mexicans' total nutrition, and almost no corn remained for animal feed.)[21] Still, only a modest share of the U.S. corn surplus was sold on the international market at the turn of the twentieth century; the chief grain imported by Europe from the United States was wheat, a trend that continued clear through to the onset of the Great Depression.

King of the Trading Pits

World War I brought changes to Americans' consumption of and later trading in corn. "Corn has occupied a most conspicuous position in the grain world," the *Chicago Daily Tribune* reported in its review of the trading annals of 1917. Because wheat (among other staples) was reserved for sending to the allies overseas, "disappointing" wheat supplies at home led to a "buying craze that seized the public," embracing most of the leading food supplies, but particularly flour. Cash wheat prices pushed skyward, "to the highest levels ever recorded in the history of the trade," and thanks to hoarders, wheat flour became both prohibitively expensive and scarce.

As reported in the *Daily Tribune*, wheat's price spike enhanced corn's appeal: "Because of the general shortage of wheat, the use of corn as human food has become more widespread." However, a small 1916 corn crop followed by a frost-damaged one in 1917 meant that the yellow grain was relatively scarce as well, as another *Daily Tribune* article makes clear: "The shortage has been pronounced during the last six months of the period and prices soared to prohibitive levels, for a time exceeding the fixed price of wheat, something never before heard of."[22]

Although most postwar homemakers gladly returned to wheat when its availability rallied back, the traders didn't forget about corn. It was a slow build, but after World War I, corn found a foothold in trading marts. Further, government intervention in wheat trading forced many traders into a cautious, watchful stance, sending many into the relatively unfettered corn market, where it was easier to speculate and profit. By 1931, a *Chicago Daily Tribune* headline trumpeted: "Corn Deposes Wheat as Ruler of Chicago Board of Trade Pits." The somewhat overly dramatic newspaper account reported, "The dynasty of wheat is at an end," further declaring, "The Board of Trade has chosen a native king." Finally, the article rounded out the hyperbole: "Ruler of the pits, these 84 years in the world's greatest grain mart, wheat will be deposed next Monday as the trade acknowledges the native maize as market leader." As a result, corn trading would be transferred into the larger pit formerly occupied by the wheat buyers and sellers, while the evicted wheat traders moved to a smaller pit. The article notes a pronounced change in trading volume, as speculators "bought and sold less than one-fourth the volume of wheat yesterday that was traded a year ago; they traded nearly four times the quantity of corn."[23]

Corn or Cattle?

As we have seen, in addition to feeding humans, corn has long been used to feed cattle. So when the Chicago Mercantile Exchange (CME) instituted cattle futures in the 1960s and 1970s, the CBOT took notice and responded by launching its own cattle contracts. Cattlemen already traded corn futures because they used corn as feed, CBOT officials reasoned, so these ranchers could stick around and hedge cattle too. However, the cattle business was already entrenched at the CME, and the CBOT eventually gave up on beef trading and went back to focusing on grain (for more on cattle trading, see chapter 7). Although the CBOT never became the cattle giant it had envisioned, by drawing cattle hedgers to the futures markets at all, corn-trading volumes increased during this period.

Big Corn

Corn was the crop that put cash in the farmer's pocket, writes Michael Pollan about corn's ascension as America's top crop.[24] The story of "Big Corn" starts back in the 1930s, when two game-changing events took place. First, commercial use of hybrid corn seed began in the United States in 1933. Hybrids dramatically increased yields, by as much as 100 percent compared with conventional seed. By 1941, 40 percent of all corn acreage used hybrid seed. The planting of hybrid seed corn became universal in the 1950s, the first seed type for which that held true.[25] The second major event was the advent of government intervention in agriculture, which began in the 1930s and continued until after World War II. Direct government subsidies, or indirect subsidies in the form of price supports, became one of the dynamic forces behind rapid agricultural growth in the postwar period. As corn yields began to soar at mid-century, the temptation was to give the miracle crop more and more land. Further encouraged by government policies, farmers nationwide shared the same thought, and although corn prices subsequently declined, more and more corn was planted.[26]

Of course, it wasn't only farmers who stood to profit; the pockets of speculators were filled with cash from the corn crop as well, particularly as it grew more and more indispensable to large corporations and agribusinesses. Corn yields increased rapidly not only with the use of hybrid seeds but with the advent of new chemical fertilizers, insecticides, and better, labor-saving machinery for planting, tending, and harvesting crops. Yields went from an average of 50 and 75 bushels an acre in the 1950s to nearly 100 in the 1960s.[27]

The flood tide of cheap corn in the 1950s and 1960s made it profitable to fatten cattle on feedlots (and corn) instead of grass, and to raise chickens in giant factories rather than on farm lots. Eventually, the chickens and cattle disappeared from the farm and, with them, the pastures, hay fields, and fences. In their place, the farmers planted the one crop they could grow more of than anything else. And whenever the price of corn slipped, they planted a little more of it, to cover expenses and stay even. By the 1980s, the diversified family farm was history in much of the American Midwest, and corn was king.[28]

It is worth noting the difference between corn, the food, and corn, the commodity—a distinction that often needs to be made with a number of traded foodstuffs. Michael Pollan sums up "number 2 field corn," the grade specified in the contract that trades on the CME. He describes it as "an internationally recognized commodity grown everywhere (and nowhere in particular), fungible, traded in and speculated upon and accepted as a form of capital all over the world." He continues: "While number 2 field corn certainly *looks* like the corn you would eat . . . it is less a food than an industrial raw material—and an abstraction. The kernels are hard to eat, but if you soak them in water for several hours you'll find they taste less like corn than lightly corn-flavored starch."[29]

Although the companies wouldn't confirm this to Michael Pollan (and denied my requests for an interview or information), it has been estimated that Cargill and Archer Daniels Midland together buy somewhere near a third of all the corn grown in the United States.[30] Further, the biggest portion of America's commodity corn (about 60 percent of it) still goes to feeding livestock, and much of that goes to feeding America's 100 million beef cattle,[31] the so-called hides stuffed with corn.

It's amazing all the different ways corn is used, in addition to the sheer delight of consuming corn straight from the cob with butter during the height of the summer harvest season. Pollan describes the multitude of uses: the kernel is subdivided, with the yellow skin processed into various vitamins and nutritional supplements; the tiny germ is crushed for oil; the endosperm is plundered for its rich cache of complex carbohydrates. Corn starch is corn's most important contribution to the industrial food chain. Chemists have learned how to break it down into hundreds of different organic compounds—acids, starches, and alcohols. And the names of these compounds will be familiar to anyone who has studied the ingredient label on a package of processed food: citric and lactic acid; glucose, fructose, and maltodextrin; ethanol (for alcoholic beverages as well as cars), sorbitol, mannitol, and xanthan gum; modified and unmodified starches; dextrins, cyclodextrins, and monosodium glutamate (MSG), to name only a few. And of course, high-fructose corn syrup.[32]

High-Fructose Corn Syrup Futures

But corn wasn't the only futures contract to trade: a derivative of corn, high-fructose corn syrup, briefly traded as well. Although sugar long held the sweetening crown, in the late 1960s, Japanese chemists "broke the sweetness barrier" (in the words of the Corn Refiners Association's official history of high-fructose corn sweetener) and discovered the enzyme that could transform glucose into much sweeter sugar molecules called fructose. By the 1970s, the process of refining corn into fructose had been perfected, and high-fructose corn syrup—which is a blend of 55 percent fructose and 45 percent glucose—came onto the market. Today, it is the most valuable food product refined from corn, accounting for 530 million bushels every year (a bushel of corn yields 33 pounds of fructose).[33] And each year, those 530 million bushels of corn are turned into 17.5 billion pounds of high-fructose corn syrup.[34]

Much changed in 1974: in November of that year, driven by falling worldwide production and dwindling stocks, raw sugar prices surged to a record 60 cents a pound, a nearly fivefold increase in a span of less than ten months. Consumers started to resist, cutting back on purchases of sugar and sugar-laden products. And then something called high-fructose corn syrup entered the fray.

The Japanese developed high-fructose corn syrup by adding an enzyme to corn starch, producing a result some experts say is twice as sweet as sugar. As sugar prices started to soar, high-fructose corn syrup began looking attractive to manufacturers, which were having trouble passing along rising sugar costs to skittish consumers.[35] With larger companies manufacturing and using high-fructose corn syrup, the need arose for a financial product to help offset the risk.

In March 1987, the U.S. Commodity Futures Trading Commission (CFTC) approved a Minneapolis Grain Exchange application to trade a futures contract in high-fructose corn syrup (HFCS).[36] However, the market lasted only two years, and the contract was shut down permanently in December 1988. According to an academic study conducted nearly ten years after the demise of the contract, 80 percent of the HFCS market was dominated by two commercial monoliths: PepsiCo and Coca-Cola USA—the only companies to trade in the contract. While "uninformed" speculative traders were the dominant participants in the HFCS futures market, a broader group of "informed" market participants never materialized to create the kind of liquidity needed to sustain active trading, which after the first year rapidly dwindled to a trading volume of nearly zero.[37] HFCS futures are now a mere footnote in trading history, though the corn-derived product still is used in a wide number of food products and remains a hot-button topic among modern food activists—testament to the importance corn plays in all manner of American foodways.

What Trades Now

- *Corn*: Trades on the CME. Contract size is 5,000 bushels (127 metric tons). There is also a "mini-size" contract that trades at 1,000 bushels (25 metric tons). The product specifies No. 2 Yellow, although No. 1 Yellow may be substituted at a 1.5 cents per bushel premium, or No. 3 Yellow, at a 1.5 cents per bushel discount.[38]
- *Distillers' Dried Grain (DDG)*: Trades on the CME. Contract size is 100 short tons (approximately 90.72 metric tons). DDG futures are the dried residue remaining after the starch fraction of corn is fermented, using selected yeasts and enzymes, to produce ethanol. After fermentation, the alcohol is removed by distillation and the remaining residues are either dried or remain wet. DDG futures are used primarily as a feed additive for cattle and dairy cows, but they also are incorporated into other livestock feed rations. Participants in this market include ethanol producers; feed merchandisers, mills, and importers/exporters; and livestock operators.[39]

"A Flurry in Wheat": the chaos of grain trading on the floor of the Chicago Board of Trade is depicted in this illustration from *Harper's New Monthly Magazine* (1880). (Courtesy of *Harper's Magazine*)

CHAPTER FOUR

Great Grains

Grain is the currency of currencies.
VLADIMIR LENIN

A statue of Ceres, the Roman goddess of grain, sits atop the historic Chicago Board of Trade (CBOT), the exchange that made its fortune in the grain business. She has presided there, forty-five stories above La Salle Street, since 1930—a time when American agriculture was crippled by drought, and the United States was forced to import wheat. At the foot of the same historic art deco building is the Ceres Café, where traders and tourists mingle over lunchtime sandwiches on whole wheat bread slices and after-work whiskeys, distilled from humble grain.

Grain trading has long been an important part of America's financial and food history. America started as a largely pastoral land, and westward expansion in the nineteenth century brought a vast acreage of farm crops to the Midwest, our fabled "amber waves of grain."

Haine's Feed Store

The earliest organized trading of that grain took place in Chicago, where in the 1840s, farmers, grain processors, brokers, and merchants would congregate at the Haine's Feed Store, on the banks of the Chicago River.

Particularly from September to November, when the harvest trade was at its peak, hundreds of farmers would bring their wares each day to Chicago, where they could receive more cash for their crops, and subsequently load up on supplies—dry goods and groceries, boots and hardware—for the return trip home. Grain and other agricultural products piled up beside the wooden buildings, while wagons, animals, mud, and manure filled the unpaved streets. For a few glorious weeks, until ice closed the harbor, the streets surrounding Haine's brimmed with a lively and chaotic trading scene.

Grain cycled through Chicago via wagon and then boat as well, particularly after the Illinois and Michigan Canal opened to traffic in April 1848. With the advent of the canal, farmers in the Illinois River Valley suddenly discovered an alternative to St. Louis as an outlet for their produce, further cementing Chicago as a center of commerce. Later, the burgeoning railroad lines, which would be built up over the following decades, would provide an even swifter way to transfer grain out of the Midwest after trading. Less than a decade after the canal was built, Chicagoans would regard the canal as "an old fogy institution."[1]

In fact, the railroad—the very vehicle that would transform Chicago into the nation's most powerful commodities metropolis—was in large part created by the farmers as well as the financiers. In 1847, Chicago's first mayor, William Butler Ogden, and banker Jonathan Young Scammon campaigned among northern Illinois farmers and merchants to promote the railroad enterprise (Ogden was the board of directors president and Scammon a member of the in-progress railroad). Many farmers—no doubt thinking of the muddy roads that caused them so much trouble in bringing crops to market—came forward to subscribe, even though, as Scammon remarked, "They had to borrow the first instalment of two dollars and fifty cents on share, and get trusted 'till after the harvest' for the same." Ogden reportedly managed to gather $20,000 worth of subscriptions in a single day from farmers who were selling their fall harvests on the streets of Chicago. By the following April, more than twelve hundred people had pledged to buy stock. Construction of the first thirty-one miles of the Galena and Chicago Union Railroad started in March 1848.[2] A big improvement over prairie roads, the railroad with its westward extension into Illinois's chief grain-farming region meant that more and more of the city's wheat began to arrive by rail. By 1852, more than half the city's wheat came in via the Galena and Chicago Union.[3] In 1860, Chicago received almost a hundred times more wheat by rail than wagon; and ten years after that, no one even bothered to keep statistics on the latter.[4]

The railroad encouraged producers to expand their expectations about the scale of the grain trade; grain shipments were no longer measured in individual "sacks," but rather as railcar loads consisting of about 325 bushels each.

As the railroad accelerated the flow of goods to the people who would become the buyers and sellers of the goods, the arrival of the telegraph in 1848 would speed up the flow of information. Messages that had once taken weeks to travel between Chicago and the East Coast now took minutes and seconds—and commodity prices were among the most important bits of information that traveled the wires. Thanks to the telegraph, the eastern and western markets began to move more closely in tandem than ever before, and those with the best access to telegraph news were often in a superior position to gauge the future movement of prices. Railroad and telegraph systems would expand in unison, often following the same routes. Together, they created the basis for financial markets, which would require both goods and information to facilitate trade.

"To-Arrive" Contracts

Because bread was near the center of most American and European diets, wheat was the classic cash crop of western farming. Highly popular in most early frontier communities, it brought the best market prices of any grain, and was a ready source of income in a way that corn was not (unless first converted to pork or alcohol).

As the young American nation spread westward, the economy began to engage in national and international trade—primarily in grain, which grew easily in the vast and fertile midwestern soil. The early nineteenth century saw some chaos in trade arrangements between farmers and urban grain merchants. Farmers would grow their grain in the prairies of the Midwest and, having harvested, would haul wagonloads of grain to the merchants in Chicago. This created a dramatic oversupply during the autumn, with insufficient available buyers. As a consequence, grain frequently went unsold in the city, and large quantities were either dumped in the streets or tipped into Lake Michigan.

Not unexpectedly, during the late winter and spring, when available stores were short and the lakes and waterways frozen, the supply of grain was insufficient to meet the demand of a growing urban population, and the price of grain soared. Meanwhile, trading began on a new invention known as "to-arrive" contracts, also called futures, which had started among British exchanges a couple of years earlier. The contracts permitted farmers to lock in the price and deliver the grain later. This allowed the farmer to store the grain either on the farm or at a storage facility nearby and deliver it to Chicago months later. The CBOT would not establish official rules until after the Civil War, but the new contracts were a critical breakthrough, and they helped stabilize grain prices by allowing the market to anticipate the harvest.[5]

Farmers therefore began to sell crops in advance of harvest, or they sold grain stored on their farms. Deliveries to Chicago could thus be scheduled to meet demand and realistic prices obtained. Millers, merchants, and shippers could likewise plan on constant supplies of grain being available throughout the year. Clearly, such an arrangement required a high degree of organization and marketing discipline, which was provided by the to-arrive contracts and later by the trading of futures contracts.

Futures contracts had the advantage of to-arrive contracts in that the quality of delivered grain was standardized, the deliveries were enforced, the terms of payment were unified, and the prices, once agreed upon, could be disseminated widely. And the contracts themselves were acceptable as trading instruments, which gave flexibility to the holder in that the holder was not required to take delivery.[6] Consider also the impact of the Industrial Revolution: as more workers moved from farms to factories, they could no longer raise food to feed themselves. This demand for food, in turn, increased the need for shipping grain and other foodstuffs—and for managing the risks associated with that activity. Organized to-arrive trading became even more important.

At the same time, on the other side of the Atlantic in the United Kingdom, significant change was taking place—the repeal in 1846 of the Corn Laws, which had been instituted by Charles II to impose levies on imported grain. London soon became the center of the world's grain trade, with much of that grain emanating from the United States.

Grain was commonly shipped before it was sold. Shipping presented a new set of risks because a storm could delay or prevent altogether the planned arrival of grain on which a loan had been advanced by a bank. Futures trading developed as a mechanism to offset this risk.[7] According to most experts, it was the confluence of to-arrive contracts and standardized, interchangeable elevator receipts that made the futures market possible.

Futures trading also opened up opportunities for a new group of buyers and sellers that had no role in producing or any specific need of grain. These were the grain speculators, who focused on exploiting price fluctuations in the hope of making a profit. With the arrival of these speculators, the market evolved into a market not in grain itself but in the *price* of grain. "In the business centre of Chicago," wrote a bemused visitor in 1880, "you see not even one 'original package' of the great cereals."[8] The same sentence could be written about the futures market today. These speculators trading grain elevator receipts were the predecessors of the speculative futures traders we know today—and some would draw a direct line from Haine's Feed Store to the creation of the Chicago Board of Trade.

The Chicago Board of Trade

In 1848, the Chicago Board of Trade was organized to handle grain trading. Its origins were humble: eighty-two members, drawn from a wide range of occupations, gathered on South Water Street, along the bank of the Chicago River, and set to work creating the CBOT. In the beginning, it had no specific commodities focus. Its principal goals were to monitor and promote the city's commercial activity, and to resolve any disputes that might arise among its members. Like boards of trade and chambers of commerce then emerging in other U.S. cities, it sought to represent the collective voice of business interests in the city.

One of its earliest activities related to the grain trade was an impetus to improve Chicago's inspection and measurement systems. Grain elevators, which mechanized the handling of large quantities of grain in a continuously moving stream, made the old measure of grain volume (a bushel of standard size) obsolete. Starting in 1854, the CBOT pressed city merchants to institute a new, weight-based bushel that could be used to calibrate elevator scales.

For the first five years of its existence, attendance at board meetings was sparse. Officers made a constant effort to hold daily meetings to encourage trading at a single location; however, sometimes only a handful of traders showed. Organizers proffered a "sumptuous" free lunch of cheese, cakes, and beer to attract grain merchants to the floor. But Chicago's grain markets remained as decentralized as ever, with traders conducting their transactions in offices, warehouses, and streets all around the city.

Eventually, business did improve. The catalyst was a surge in European demand for grain during the Crimean War. American wheat exports doubled in volume and tripled in value during 1853 and 1854, while domestic prices rose by more than 50 percent.[9] And in Chicago, the total amount of grain exported more than tripled. Suddenly, the idea of a centralized marketplace seemed a more convenient way of doing business, and traders—usually working on commission for owners and purchasers—brought samples to the CBOT meeting room, haggled over prices, and arranged contracts among buyers and sellers, creating a single market. By 1856, membership numbered in the hundreds. CBOT leaders even felt confident enough to discontinue their "sumptuous" refreshments. Daily meetings on the floor of what was beginning to be called the 'Change (short for "Exchange") soon became so crowded that the board moved to new quarters on the corner of La Salle and South Water Streets.

One of the CBOT's first challenges was dealing with the grain elevator dilemma. While the elevators, which were capable of moving vast quantities of corn and grain, had liberated producers from trading by the mere sackful, they now posed a storage problem. Grain from various producers commingled in large bins and on railcars. Farmers and shippers delivered grain to a warehouse and got in return a receipt that they or anyone else could redeem at will. Anyone who presented an elevator receipt for grain got in return not the original lot of grain but an equal quantity of like grain. Those elevator receipts effectively created a new form of money, as the receipts traded on the floor of the 'Change. It was a momentous transformation. As one visitor to Chicago remarked after a tour of one of the elevators, "It dawns on the observer's mind that one man's property is by no means kept separate from another man's."[10]

The problem was elevators had no reliable way to grade and separate grains of different quality as they entered the warehouse. Chicago's grain developed a poor reputation among eastern buyers for being particularly poor quality. It was a "common occurrence" for farmers to send damp and dirty grain to market, while country shippers were accused of "mixing at times oats, rye, barley screenings or samp [chopped dried corn kernels] and unmerchantable wheat with that of sound and good quality."[11] Worried that such reports would soon hurt its market, between 1857 and 1859 the board introduced a series of reforms, providing standards for grain quality (and later for barley, corn, oats, and rye as well). Grains were ranked by quality (No. 1, No. 2, and so on) and by type (spring wheat, winter wheat, and so on). These grades made it possible for traders to buy and sell grain as an abstract claim on the city's elevator, rather than as individual physical sacks. It made the grains interchangeable between elevator bins but also between cities and even continents. Grading commodities for the purposes of quality assurance is standard practice in the industry today.

Although several trading hubs sprung up in southern mercantile cities, when the Civil War started, many merchants in Cincinnati, St. Louis, and other cities with a long-standing tradition of southern trade shut down their firms and moved to Chicago. By the end of 1861, eight hundred members made the CBOT a thriving center of commerce.[12]

"Old Hutch" and Young Leiter

In the years following the Civil War, the futures market came to fruition — and so did the "corner." (A "corner" creates a temporary, artificial shortage that backs traders into a "corner," forcing them to pay exorbitant prices to buy back contracts representing the commodity. A mild corner was termed a "squeeze.") Alfred Andreas, Chicago's leading nineteenth-century historian, remembered 1868 as "the year of corners." "Scarcely a month" went by, he wrote, "without a corner on 'Change. Three on wheat, two on corn, one on oats, and one attempted on rye."[13] Indeed, some complained that when the CBOT changed buildings following the great Chicago fire of 1871, the tenor of trading was transformed as well. "Up to this time," grumbled one observer in 1905, "the character of the board was that of an association of men of quiet and regular business habits, whose operations lay unexcitingly along the ordinary grooves of commerce."[14] In the new era, speculation (or "plunging," as this writer derisively termed it) took deeper root. And it was around this period that the newspapers, gleefully covering fortunes rapidly made and lost, repeated the outraged public's new nickname for the Board of Trade: the "Board of Thieves." Reflecting this sense of infamy is a description of a typical trading scene at the Board of Trade:

> To the first visitor in the gallery the alarming impression is that of a wild, many-sided, free-for-all battle or series of battles between hosts of raging lunatics. Men, young and old, struggle towards each other yelling fiercely and shaking their fists and fingers, and suddenly stopping, as if at the crucial moment of conflict and slaughter, to scribble furiously on cards . . . the brokers . . . frantically shout and gesticulate, all facing inward, giving the idea that some poignantly-interesting encounter, dreadful manslaughter or red murder, is being perpetrated. The largest is the celebrated and historic wheat pit, a commercial maelstrom in which many a golden fortune has been made and lost. . . . On the west side are about a hundred telegraphers, making a noise like a continuous rattle of musketry; they are kept busy during trading hours receiving and sending messages. . . . Messenger boys rush about, and the floor is yellow with torn telegrams, lying thick as autumn leaves.[15]

Amid this backdrop, two grain-corner stories in particular read almost like fables: the story of Benjamin Hutchinson, also known as "Old Hutch," the first man to corner the wheat market in a big way in the 1880s, and a much younger man, Joseph Leiter, who made a similar, if flashier, attempt just two decades later.

"Old Hutch" was a farm boy from Massachusetts who worked his way up through the trading business. He was described as "more than six feet tall, lean and angular, with large hands and feet, eyes cold and clear, a prominent hooked nose, and thin, beardless lips."[16] He went into the meatpacking business in Chicago, became a banker, formed the Corn Exchange Bank, intended to supply credit to the grain trade, and eventually became a member of the CBOT. Hutchinson was known as the king of the wheat pit, and he had a throne—a wicker chair—on the trading floor.

In 1888, Hutchinson led his most famous corner. He stealthily bought up wheat futures contracts. In the fall, a frost killed off a portion of the year's wheat crop. This worked to Hutchinson's advantage, making wheat even harder to get. Despite sellers' being wise to his plotting, there was little they could do. The market headed skyward. Showing off, Hutchinson had his broker buy 1 million bushels in a single trade. When the contract expired, sellers were unable to find wheat to deliver. They were forced to buy back futures contracts directly from Hutchinson. He made millions on the deal and embarrassed his son, who was then president of the CBOT. When the corner was over, the price of wheat crashed.

In the end, Old Hutch got his comeuppance. In 1891, he bought 3 million bushels of corn, due for delivery in July. But he didn't buy enough corn to successfully corner the market. The price dropped, which made the futures contracts he had bought worth less than he paid. He lost $2 million. His son settled his trading debts for him, and Old Hutch left for New York City. He rented a tiny office on Wall Street and slept in a swivel chair—a far cry from his trading room "throne." In an article he wrote for the *North American Review*, he argued that there could never be another big, successful corner in wheat and compared the market to Niagara Falls, something men could influence but never truly control.[17]

Just a few years later, a younger man would try to become the new wheat king. In 1897, twenty-eight-year-old Harvard graduate Joseph Leiter was the equivalent of a modern-day trust-fund kid. He was possessed of considerable charm and fortune—a flamboyant dandy known for his trademark white waistcoat and pearl-gray stovepipe hat—and succeeded in sailing his own yacht around the world. Leiter's wealth was inherited from his father, Levi Z. Leiter, copartner of Chicago's Marshall Field's department store, who later turned to banking, real estate, and land development. The junior Leiter had started in business with $1 million from his father, earmarked for starting a real-estate firm. Land speculation proved too slow for Leiter's taste. He instead turned to the thrill of the commodities market. He started buying wheat futures. The Indian and European crops had been poor, and Chicago prices rose steadily. Leiter kept buying, leaving the sellers with larger and larger commitments to deliver this wheat to Chicago. Like Old Hutch before him, Leiter was planning to corner the wheat market.

Unfortunately for Leiter, the person on the other side of his wheat corner was veteran trader Philip D. Armour, a self-made man who was not amused by this upstart's brazen efforts. Peedee, as he was known, was a former Milwaukee meat packer who made his fortune during the Civil War by speculating on then-scarce pork. In 1875, the forty-three-year-old Armour moved to Chicago, where he became the city's largest owner of grain elevators and founder of Armour & Company, which would become the biggest meatpacking firm in a city of meat packers. Although some midwestern farmers were delighted by the rising price of wheat—many lit candles in his honor[18]—Armour, now in his sixties, resolved to put the whippersnapper in his place.

For a while, Leiter's corner worked magnificently. He began buying in April 1897. By early December, Armour was "short"—that is, he had sold—9 million bushels of wheat, and due largely to Leiter's aggressive importing, Armour had fewer than 350,000 bushels in his Chicago grain elevators. But that would change. Anticipating the onset of winter, Armour sent men throughout the Northwest, encouraging farmers to sweep their barns to find every last kernel. Finally, with the help of Minneapolis elevator king Frank Peavy, Armour had enough wheat.

Now the challenge was beating the brutal winter—if the northern waterways froze, he would be unable to ship wheat to Chicago. Armour directed huge quantities of wheat into Chicago, and as the Great Lakes routes from Duluth, Minnesota, and Ontario, Canada, began to freeze, he kept the waterways open for his vessels by dynamiting passages through the ice. He met all of his commitments, and prices fell. Leiter held on through the spring. However, by May, he began to sell wheat, quietly, thanks in no small part to his father's sudden appearance in Chicago. By June, the federal government predicted a record wheat crop—and wheat prices collapsed, leaving Leiter holding enormous quantities of overpriced wheat. Some estimates have him losing almost $20 million. Leiter never traded in the futures markets again.[19]

The Only Successful Corner

Throughout American history, wheat has been one of the highest-volume and most highly speculative markets, spurring more than its fair share of trading scandals in New York and Chicago in the nineteenth century. Illicit "bucket shops" thrived—tiny one-room outfits set up with phones and little else, with the sole purpose of exploiting swings in prices, often by unlawful means. Grain-related plays were a bucket-shop mainstay.

While bucket shops in stocks flourished in the East, the most vigorous growth occurred in the less financially sophisticated Midwest. At the height of the bucket-shop boom, twenty-five such outfits operated in the immediate vicinity of the Board of Trade; more than one hundred were in the city.[20] In 1905, after years of lengthy legal battles in appellate courts, the U.S. Supreme Court ruled that commodities exchanges were legitimate entities and bucket shops were not.[21] Eventually, outlawed by state and local statutes, and harassed by the newspapers and souring public opinion, the gambling-oriented bucket shops disappeared.

With bucket shops under control and Leiter's attempt to corner the market fading into memory, James A. Patten came along in 1908 and by 1909 had orchestrated perhaps the only successful major market corner in the Board of Trade's history. The son of a politically well-connected family in Chicago's far south suburb of Sandwich, Patten was one of the most prominent traders on the board. He had run a corner on oats in 1902, prompting several bills in Congress to outlaw short selling and other speculative practices. But the 1909 wheat corner made Patten a household name: he was vilified in sermons and caricatured in editorial cartoons.

The corner began in June 1908, with wheat trading at around 90 cents a bushel. Before the deal was done, Patten would buy 10 million bushels and drive up the price of wheat to $1.34 by the end of May 1909, the highest price since Leiter's corner. Patten's profits were estimated at more than $1 million. Whatever the profit, the corner exacted a price. The pressure from Washington was intense. A bill was introduced to prohibit futures trading, and an investigation into Patten's dealings was launched. Secretary of Agriculture James Wilson blamed Patten for artificially raising the price of wheat when he claimed supplies were plentiful.

No legislation resulted directly from the Patten corner, but for decades, his name would be held up when discussion arose about the need for government regulation of the markets. At the height of the Patten panic, the newspapers brooded over fear of bread riots in Chicago's immigrant neighborhoods. "Why, a woman can't fill a pincushion with bran without taking Jim Patten into account," jabbed *Worker's Magazine*.[22]

The End of the Golden Grain Era

Dramatic market corners aside, the grain business continued to prosper. In 1930, at the foot of La Salle Street, the Board of Trade members erected a joyful art deco edifice as its headquarters, the tallest building in the city, crowned with the thirty-one-foot-tall aluminum statue of Ceres, holding a sheaf of wheat in her left hand and a bag of corn in her right. (The CME Group put the historic landmark building up for sale in June 2011.)

Grain trading never ceased, but it suffered a significant hit in the 1930s, when the Great Depression began and governments became heavily involved in setting price controls. Wily traders looked to other, less regulated markets, such as meat and soybeans, to make their mark. Even for those who stuck to the grain market, the balance of contracts changed. Although wheat, corn, and oats have held steady as staple contracts throughout the decades, trading in other grains and oilseeds has fluctuated. Trading in barley and rye, both active contracts in the 1930s, gave way to sorghum, millfeed, and flaxseed in the 1950s. By 1980, soybeans, soybean meal, and soybean oil were among the most active contracts (for information about the soybean phenomenon, see chapter 10).[23]

A Second Gold Rush in California

Although the Midwest gets all the attention as the center of grain growing and trading, the amber waves of grain also played a key role in California. Once gold rush fever abated there, enterprising newcomers found that wheat grew well in the fertile Sacramento and San Joaquin Valleys. They staked out ranches and began growing wheat. As railroads started penetrating farther west, the volumes of marketable wheat increased.

However, the transcontinental railroads were not yet built, and it was difficult to transport wheat to the populous, ravenous Eastern Seaboard cities. So California farmers began to export to foreign countries by boat. England became the primary market for California wheat, and by 1870, California had become so dependent on the English market that it used a British measurement (the cental: 100 pounds) instead of the bushel. "California No. 1" was a standard grain variety traded at the Liverpool Corn Trade Association in the 1880s. A running joke maintained that there were only two subjects of conversation on the wheat ranches: "the weather in California and the price of wheat in Liverpool."[24]

"In two months alone in 1841 there arrived in London 787 vessels from foreign ports, laden with foreign corn ["corn" was still used as a catchall for various grains]," recounted author Walter Thornbury, "a fact which proves the ceaseless cry for bread of hungry England, unable to fully supply its own wants, and dependent on the energy of the Mark Lane dealers."[25]

Just as the Pillsburys and Cargills made their names in grain in the Midwest, the undisputed California "Grain King" was Isaac Friedlander, a speculator who amassed a fortune cornering wheat and sailing vessels in San Francisco, only to lose it all in 1877 and then die just one year later. By the end of the century, competition from new producers, such as Argentina, Australia, and Canada, forced prices lower. California's wheat exports dwindled rapidly, and as wheat sprouted quickly across the plains and prairies of the Midwest, the luster of California's golden crops began to dim.

Nevertheless, commodities marts sprung up along the West Coast, proving that wheat could be as speculative as gold. The Los Angeles Grain Exchange and San Francisco Grain Exchange each opened in 1922 (the latter closed in 1938, according to the U.S. Commodity Futures Trading Commission, while the former stuck it out until 1945). Farther north, the Seattle Grain Exchange made markets from 1926 until 1959, while the Portland Grain Exchange was open from 1929 through 1942.[26]

Forgotten Grain Exchanges

By the early twentieth century, the two Chicago exchanges had more or less divided up the contracts. The venerable CBOT traded grains such as wheat, corn, oats, rye, and barley, as well as soybeans and cotton. Meanwhile, the grittier CME, which began life as an egg-and-butter board, became the go-to exchange for livestock futures, including cattle, hogs, and fresh broilers, as well as what remained of egg and dairy futures.

Perhaps more so than any other agricultural commodity traded in the United States, grain has long been sold on myriad local exchanges around the country, consolidating decade by decade into the monolith exchanges we know today. In 1931, grains and/or oilseed products (e.g., soybeans and flaxseed) traded on at least thirteen exchanges, including the Duluth Board of Trade, the Omaha Grain Exchange, the Portland Grain Exchange, and the San Francisco Grain Exchange. By 1955, that number dwindled to nine, including the Memphis Board of Trade, the Milwaukee Grain Exchange, the New York Produce Exchange, the Seattle

TRADING WHISKEY

Perhaps the most exciting—and notorious—by-product of grain is whiskey. As long as Americans have had access to grain, we have found a way to distill and consume it as alcohol. We have also found myriad ways to sell, trade, and tax alcohol.

Early listings of trade provisions in newspapers usually included an account of whiskey prices. On the opening day for New York's Produce Exchange, the *New York Times* published a trade table listing, among other products, 1,010 barrels of whiskey at 19 cents a gallon.[*]

The Whiskey Trust

As contracts began to formalize on the exchanges, whiskey soon dropped out of the market listings, and "The Whiskey Trust" took control of alcohol pricing. In the last two decades of the nineteenth century, the "trust" became a legal shelter for commercial combinations, in many ways the forerunner of the modern corporate structure. The device of the trust came into general use after the Standard Oil Company had developed it as a means of eliminating competitors. As taxation on the liquor industry increased, dampening drinking activity, whiskey makers banded together to create a trust, in the hope of controlling the industry. "We thought," said distiller Charles C. Clarke, of Peoria, Illinois, "we could make better profits and create a more stable business by organizing into a trust. A trust agreement was drawn up, which was a copy of the Standard Oil trust agreement, but changed to suit our business."[†] The Trust handled about two-thirds of the beverage alcohol consumed in the United States during the late 1880s and 1890s.

An essential feature of the agreement was laid out in this way: shares of stock in corporations that formerly competed were placed in the hands of trustees who thereafter operated the combination as a single unit. But ultimately, the trust closed down most of the distilleries it acquired, and price-fixing was rampant. The trust would lower the price of whiskey to force independent distillers into the organization; later, the price would skyrocket, and the trust would reap a harvest.

The trust went into and out of receivership a number of times, accompanied by slight changes to its corporate name and the sloughing off of inconvenient financial obligations. Sometimes the Whiskey Trust was the American Spirits Manufacturing Company or the Standard Distilling and Distributing Company—or it might dissolve altogether into the Distillers'

Securities Corporation, a holding company incorporated under New Jersey's hospitable laws. And during the purportedly dry Prohibition years, the trust transformed into U.S. Food Products Corporation, making yeast, vinegar, and cereal products.[‡]

An incarnation of the Whiskey Trust continues today. In 1924, the trust reinvented itself again as the National Distillers Products Corporation. Under the leadership of Seton Porter, a man with no whiskey background, National Distillers proceeded to buy up priceless stocks of whiskey that lay fallow during the Prohibition years—and by the repeal of Prohibition in 1933, the company owned more than half the aged whiskey in the United States.[§] In 1950, National Distillers acquired US Industrial Chemicals (at the time, one of the largest and oldest industrial chemical concerns, and ironically, incorporated in 1906 as the US Industrial Alcohol Company, a maker of alcohol "for industrial and medicinal purposes"). In 1988, the combined entity changed its name to Quantum Chemical Corporation, now one of the largest U.S. producers and marketers of propane gas and other petrochemicals. The company no longer makes whiskey or any other alcoholic beverage.

The American Liquor Exchange

During the last days of Prohibition, as Seton Porter surely was assessing his vast whiskey stores, a group of distillers and importers gathered in a paneled office overlooking Park Avenue in New York. As liquor returned to legal status, this group, founded by importer Sidney Reich, created the American Liquor Exchange.

Technically, this group was not an exchange, but a firm dealing in warehouse receipts. This financial instrument pledged as collateral specific barrels of whiskey (and other spirits) in a government warehouse. The contents of each precious barrel, unlike most commodities, rose constantly in value, according to age, the percentage of small grain used, the quality of the original distillation, the district of origin, and the demand for particular blocks of whiskey. The receipts were generally regarded as a prime investment. (Warehouse receipts were not specific to the liquor industry. In fact, warehouse receipts representing massive amounts of soybean and cottonseed oil would play a key role in what would become the "Great Salad Oil Swindle," explained in detail in chapter 10.)

However, in some ways it was very much like a traditional exchange. An Associated Press photo shows what appears to be an auction; a broker with

In this rare photograph, members of the American Liquor Exchange set post-Prohibition prices for wine and spirits (1933). (Courtesy of Ryan Carlson)

neatly slicked hair waves a finger in the air to indicate his bid; an auctioneer in a three-piece suit, standing before a microphone, acknowledges the bid and appears ready to write it down. Behind him, a chalkboard lists the bid/ ask prices for various whiskeys—rye, Scotch—as well as other spirits (gin, Cognac, "Cuban rhum") and Champagne and other wines. The asking price for Johnny Walker Black Label is $26.50 for a quantity of fifteen hundred cases (a bottle of the same blended Scotch retails for roughly $35 a bottle these days). Reich estimated for the United Press syndicate that there was $2.6 million in buying power in the office looking for whiskey. Meanwhile, the available stock was about 40,000 gallons, which represented $350,000 at current prices. Most of the deals called for delivery in thirty, sixty, or ninety days after the repeal went into effect.°°

Because there are very few mentions of the American Liquor Exchange after its initial launch, it is difficult to say how long the entity lasted as a mechanism for setting liquor prices. If it lasted until the 1940s, most likely the exchange was disbanded during World War II. For its part, during World War II, National Distillers turned its attention from drinking-alcohol to industrial alcohol and chemicals, a more lucrative and pressing industry during wartime. The task of pricing whiskey likely returned to the hands of distillers, importers, and retailers during the postwar years, which is the structure that remains in place today.

However, we may not have seen the end of whiskey as a financial instrument. Similar to wine investment, a small but vocal group is talking about buying and selling whiskey, particularly rare and old Scotches, as an alternative investment strategy. Certainly, the stratospheric prices fetched at auctions in the past year or so support this idea. Advocates are starting to refer to "investment-grade whiskey" and use the Whisky Highland Index, newly established in 2011, to track potential valuations. CNBC reported that even the Whisky Exchange (a British-based spirits importer/exporter, not a recognized commodities exchange) is looking to establish a whiskey investment fund in 2012.[††] Surely, curious investors around the world will be watching carefully, eager to learn if grain in the form of rare whiskey constitutes "liquid gold."

*"General Markets," New York Times, April 22, 1861.

†Quoted in Gerald Carson, The Social History of Bourbon (Lexington: University Press of Kentucky, 2010), 128–129.

‡Ibid., 134–135.

§Ibid.

**Max Buckingham, "Liquor Dealings Flourishing in New York but Epidemic of Parched Throats Goes On," United Press, October 7, 1933.

††"Alternative Investing: Whiskey," CNBC video, December 13, 2011, http://video.cnbc.com/gallery/?video=3000062138 (accessed April 4, 2012).

Grain Exchange, and the St. Louis Mercantile Exchange. And by 1980, the count had diminished to four: the Chicago Board of Trade, the Kansas City Board of Trade, the Mid-America Commodity Exchange, and the Minneapolis Grain Exchange.[27] Added to that count is the New Orleans Commodity Exchange, which began trading rice futures in March 1981 and lasted for a full year before shutting its doors.[28]

Many of these exchanges have now been lost to history, forgotten even by most local denizens and market participants. Over time, improvements in communications and trading technology and the enhanced liquidity of a larger, centralized trading community have resulted in relentless exchange consolidation. Only two independent exchanges remain, albeit primarily in electronic format: the Kansas City Board of Trade still trades hard red winter wheat (a hearty strain brought to Kansas by immigrants from the southern Russian steppes, primarily used to make bread; it is also a key ingredient in Maker's Mark whiskey) and the Minneapolis Board of Trade deals in hard red spring wheat (a high-protein variety, also primarily milled for bread, and the continent's most widely exported wheat). "Winter" and "spring" refer to when the varieties are planted.

The exchange landscape narrowed even further in 2007, when the Chicago Board of Trade and the Chicago Mercantile Exchange merged in a $11.9 billion deal, creating the CME Group, the world's largest futures and options market, and ending two centuries of sparring and rivalry between the two exchanges. A *Forbes* article summed up the end of the era neatly: "The fat lady finally sang."[29]

What Trades Now

- *Wheat*: Trades on the CME. Contract size is 5,000 bushels (about 127 metric tons); a "mini-size" contract (1,000 bushels) also trades. Deliverable grades include No. 2 Soft Red Winter Wheat, No. 1 Soft Red Winter Wheat, and No. 2 Dark Northern Spring.[30]
- *Oats*: Trades on the CME. Contract size is 5,000 bushels.[31]
- *Rough Rice*: Trades on the CME. Long-grain rice. Contract size is 2,000 hundredweight.[32]
- *Hard Red Winter Wheat*: Trades on the Kansas City Board of Trade. Futures contract size is 5,000 bushels.[33]
- *Hard Red Spring Wheat*: Trades on the Minneapolis Grain Exchange. Futures contract size is 5,000 bushels.[34]

Egg traders handle the merchandise at the Chicago Mercantile Exchange (1949). (Image used with the permission of CME Group Inc. © 2011. All rights reserved.)

CHAPTER FIVE

Butter-and-Egg Men

And though consumers feast or fast
Your butter'n'egg men laugh the last!
CHICAGO DAILY NEWS, OCTOBER 1919

In Manhattan's Duane Park sits a bench with a worn, engraved plaque: "Reserved For the Ghosts of Commerce." Among the ghosts that haunt this now highly gentrified stretch of Tribeca were the humble dairy dealers known as the butter-and-egg men. It may seem hard to envision now, in the age of refrigerated trucks and ice-making machines, but there was a time when eggs and dairy products were highly perishable and precious. And the traders who dealt in contracts related to those products were the comfortable "butter-and-eggers," wealthy but crude, who liked to joke that their wives were fat because they buttered their toast on both sides.

Talk to many old-timers today, and they recall the days when the Merc was once "a butter-and-egg exchange." Some remember those days fondly; for others, it is a memory of a limping exchange before it was revitalized in the early 1960s. Regardless, most agree that the old butter-and-egg market was an important stepping-stone to the modern exchange. As the wheat market led to the creation of the Chicago Board of Trade, the butter-and-egg market led directly to the creation of the rival Chicago Mercantile Exchange as well as New York's own Mercantile Exchange.

A Tale of Two Cities

In 1872, dairy merchants split off from the New York Produce Exchange and founded the Butter and Cheese Exchange of New York.[1] With the addition of eggs, it was named the Butter, Cheese, and Egg Exchange, and by 1882, the organization was renamed yet again, becoming the New York Mercantile Exchange as trade broadened to include dried fruits, canned goods, and poultry.

In New York, the area now known as tony Tribeca (the triangle below Canal Street)—north of Chambers Street and east of Greenwich Street—was once the butter, cheese, and egg section of the city, populated by middlemen who would bring in barrelfuls of eggs from local farms, cushioned by oats, and sell to New York's stores and restaurants. "The butter and egg men were members of the New York Mercantile Exchange," remembers writer Michael Shapiro, painting a detailed picture of a day in the life of his grandfather's butter-and-egg business:

> Every weekday morning they left their stores and walked around the corner to the redbrick exchange building where at 10:30 precisely they performed the ritual of setting the price of eggs for the nation. Then they walked back to their stores, along impossibly narrow streets crowded with trucks and with men doing the lifting and hauling that many of the wealthy butter and egg men had themselves done when they had first come to the trade. Their stores were narrow and deep and generally filled with little more than a desk, a phone, tubs of butter and thousands of eggs. They spent their days selling to restaurants, stores, ocean liners, each other and, for a while anyway, that newest form of retailing, the supermarkets.[2]

The old egg men began to recede after their produce counterparts on the other side of Greenwich Street were moved to Hunts Point in the Bronx in 1967. The rise of huge distribution networks—supermarkets and industrial farms—changed the way business was conducted in a sweeping way.[3] Butter and eggs became part of the agribusiness complex; former produce warehouses were turned into expensive lofts for celebrity tenants. One by one, New York's butter-and-egg men, those "ghosts of commerce," left lower Manhattan behind.

Meanwhile, Chicago, the nation's dairy land, saw much more activity, and became the trading hub. In the 1880s, the Produce Exchange Butter and Egg Board splintered off from the existing Chicago Produce Exchange, forming the Chicago Butter and Egg Board in 1898. About two decades later, in 1919, this group reorganized itself to become the Chicago Mercantile Exchange, with the forward-looking thought that it might become desirable to trade in other commodities as well as in butter-and-egg futures.

But even before those exchanges were formed, in its earliest days, the produce business was merely a kitchen-garden offshoot of the mighty midwestern grain machine. Compared with the polished robber barons of the midwestern grain machine, the merchants who dealt in produce were more likely to be newly arrived immigrants, struggling to build a family business. Produce by nature was perishable and, with the exception of eggs, was not storable or suitable for future delivery. In fact, were it not for the role played by eggs, Chicago's produce business probably would have remained a local market.

As with grain, Chicago had become a transit point for eggs. Nearly every midwestern farm had a few laying hens, and farmers' wives carried their eggs into the nearest town to barter for other merchandise. Local merchants often accepted the eggs as a courtesy to the farm wives; they then packed the eggs off to Chicago, where dealers sold them to restaurateurs and wholesaler grocers or arranged transit to egg-consuming markets in the Northeast or the South.

Eggs at the time were a seasonal crop, with most of the production occurring in the early spring. Before refrigeration, butter, cheese, and other dairy products were also seasonal. Dairy products were relatively scarce in winter months. They became more plentiful in the spring as calving season arrived and cows gave greater amounts of milk. Prices frequently rose in the summer, as the heat of the sun quickly spoiled perishable dairy products.

For Chicago dealers, arranging year-round contracts in the country was important business. Each February, these butter-and-egg men (a Broadway show of the time mirrored this moniker with the title *Butter and Egg Man*) would invite their humble country suppliers to a dinner at the Sherman Hotel in downtown Chicago. After priming the rubes with lavish amounts of food and spirits, the city brokers would haul out contracts that committed the country folks to deliver set carloads of eggs at particular times during the year.

These forward contracts fluctuated in value. However, delivery on the agreements was dismal, with country suppliers often refusing to ship if the price had risen in the intervening period and Chicago dealers refusing to pay when spot prices dropped below the forward price. There was no clearinghouse for the contracts and no way to enforce delivery.

These chronic problems contributed to the revival of the Chicago Produce Exchange in 1884, after eight years of inactivity. The first Chicago trade organization that prominently featured butter and eggs, the Chicago Produce Exchange had been organized on May 20, 1874. The born-again exchange—an agglomeration of produce dealers, egg traders, and oleomargarine dealers—published a set price for butter and eggs at the end of each day.

However, the butter-and-egg dealers grew dissatisfied with the exchange and the way it allowed its secretary to determine prices by querying merchants in a haphazard way. In 1895, dealers formed the Produce Exchange Butter and Egg Board as part of the Chicago Produce Exchange, its only purpose being to provide a better way to determine butter and egg prices. But in the next couple of years, the exchange suffered from a civil war, as the butter merchants battled with their hated rivals, the margarine men, or oleo faction. The butter merchants tried to use the exchange to influence state legislators to limit the sale of margarine in Illinois. The oleo producers thwarted them. As a result of the dissension, on February 8, 1898, the butter-and-egg men withdrew from the Chicago Produce Exchange, forming their own organization: the Chicago Butter and Egg Board, destined to one day become the Merc.[4]

This anonymous poem, which uses humor to acknowledge the power of the Merc's butter-and-egg men, appeared in the *Chicago Daily News* in 1919:

> Hail, noble shell of busy trade
> In butter, also eggs fresh laid,
> Or else, in pristine freshness stored
> In some chill, superarctic hoard,—
> Or else those eggs expected when
> It suits the mood of Mrs. Hen—
> Not egocentric in your art,
> For barnyard creatures play their part

On your façade, We see the cow,
Contentment sculptured on her brow;
The faithful hen here gets a show
Despite her lord and master's crow,
Like statesman, bard and soldier strong
The clucking bird in frozen song
Is here exalted. (If you please,
No wheeze on eggs upon the frieze.)
Hail, produce temple, multi-tiered,
Your white and sunny side upreared;
Well built to bear your workday's yoke
You've cap'talized a Nation's joke
And though consumers feast or fast
Your butter'n'egg men laugh the last![5]

Fresh, Frozen, Storage

Although fresh eggs were plentiful after the spring lay, farmers and egg packers faced the difficult challenge of finding ways to preserve eggs for use during the winter. According to one account, "Some were packed in salt, some in lime, and some were placed in tanks containing various pickling solutions. Limed and pickled eggs persisted for some time after the rise of refrigerated eggs, limed eggs being quoted on the New York market nearly to the close of the [twentieth] century. Of course the eggs so treated tasted strongly of the preservative and were quoted at substantial discounts under fresh eggs."[6] Fresh eggs remained the gold standard.

"Storage eggs" and "frozen eggs" were key components of the early egg market, trading separately from fresh eggs. ("Storage butter" was also an actively traded commodity.) Storage eggs might keep for months; frozen eggs for years. Since eggs were seasonal—fresh eggs were plentiful in spring laying months and more scarce the rest of the year—that made for optimum trading opportunities. And demand was variable. Although it was easy to predict rising demand around holiday cake-baking time, in general it was difficult to predict how many eggs housewives would buy at the store in any given week. Egg men on the street used egg futures like short-term insurance to hedge against price swings.

There isn't much existing information about how storage or frozen egg futures were handled, but *Forbes* reporter Emily Lambert cajoled a few details out of old-school Chicago egg men. Essentially, dealers would buy fresh eggs and store them "in a cooler or cold storage room in anticipation of better prices. The neighborhood was dotted with the cold storage warehouses where dealers put a light coating of vegetable oil on the eggs' shells and put them in a warehouse at thirty-eight to forty degrees, where they could last for months." When prices rose, dealers would sell the eggs to hotels, restaurants, hospitals, and other customers around town, trying to resell them for a few cents more than they had paid. Meanwhile, "frozen eggs" took the concept of egg preservation one step further. Frozen eggs started life as storage eggs, which then were sold to "egg-breaking companies."

In the egg-breaking plant, workers "flash-candled" the eggs, holding whole eggs up to a candle flame to examine them for internal defects, such as blood spots and parasites. Next,

> they placed the eggs on a conveyor belt, and women on either side stood at stainless steel tables with egg-breaking equipment. As the belt moved, each woman picked eggs off the belt, broke them open, and filled cups with the yolks and whites. Then she smelled the eggs to make sure they were good. If so, she dumped the cup into a stainless steel bucket. When the bucket was filled, another employee walked it to the "floor lady," who also smelled the eggs. If they smelled okay, she dumped them into a hopper, a large receptacle with a series of screens to catch impurities. The eggs were pumped into stainless steel vats where an agitator kept them circulating. Then a worker poured thirty pounds of egg liquid into a tin, sealed the tin with a rubber mallet, and sent it to the cooler or the freezer.

The egg-breaking companies sold the frozen eggs to bakeries as well as to pie, noodle, and mayonnaise makers.[7]

End of the Chicago Butter and Egg Board

"Storage" products were popular with grocers and consumers, especially during the months when fresh butter and eggs were not in season. But they were also popular with the government, particularly during wartime.

During World War I, storage eggs and butter were snapped up to feed the military and allies overseas. What little was still available fell into the hands of hoarders. One newspaper story's tongue-in-cheek headline conveys the sentiment of the time: "Poor Old Public Must Eat Fresh Butter and Eggs." Even after the conclusion of the Great War, storage eggs remained in short supply. "The situation simply is that only a few have storage butter or eggs, and, knowing they can't get them again, they won't sell," summarized S. Edward Davis in 1919, president of the Chicago Butter and Egg Board. "Those who have them are saving them for their favorable customers and won't sell outside of their own trade. Probably some holding on and can't be pried loose, bent on carrying them over until March 1," when spring's fresh eggs would become more plentiful.[8]

In 1917, the United States' entry into World War I caused egg prices to shoot up, and many forward contracts went unfulfilled, causing a scandal in the industry and with the public. Even as the USDA, shocked at the rapid rise in grain prices, shut down wheat futures trading on the CBOT, the tiny Butter and Egg Board's 1917 military storage-egg buy-up escaped similar draconian government intervention. But after witnessing the grain shutdown at the Board of Trade, the Butter and Egg Board leaders decided to revise their trading practices, lest inaction invite a government crackdown. The board voted unanimously to abolish deals in so-called paper eggs and paper butter, and a number of butter-and-egg dealers were indicted on charges of "conspiracy in restraint of trade"—hoarding as well as arbitrary fixing and manipulation of prices. "It was charged that the dealers had done their trading in futures not on the floor of the board but in hotels, barrooms, and cafes," the *Chicago Daily Tribune* reported. The resolutions passed by the board noted "a widespread and growing opinion among the people at large that sales of 'futures' in food products result in advancing the prices of these products," although the board refuted in the same breath that this was "a conclusion to which, however, we are not prepared to subscribe," and immediately changed all sales on butter and egg products to "spot transactions only." Further, under the new arrangement, it was agreed that "all eggs dealt in must be either on track or in warehouses, and present for immediate physical delivery if demanded."[9]

In September 1919, the Chicago Butter and Egg Board ceased to be, and in its place, the Chicago Mercantile Exchange was born. The new exchange had tougher rules and grading standards, and a new clearinghouse.

CHEESE FUTURES

In addition to butter and eggs, the CME, in 1929, began trading cheese contracts. Trading volume was not particularly robust from a historical perspective, and cheese continues to be relatively thinly traded today. Cheddar is the only cheese traded on the CME, and it is sold in 40-pound blocks and 500-pound barrels.

A second market for pricing dairy products also once flourished: by the 1870s, so-called dairy boards were established, where factory representatives and cheese dealers met and engaged in organized trading. These dairy boards and their successors evolved into the National Cheese Exchange (NCE), which was located in Green Bay, Wisconsin.

Although only a tiny share of all bulk cheese transactions occurred on the NCE, this trading activity is significant because it served as a primary price-discovery mechanism for bulk cheese transactions. In fact, the NCE is infamous for its checkered history as an instrument for manipulating dairy

The new Merc offered futures and forward contracts in eggs and butter only. In 1929, cheese futures were added, and potato futures launched two years later.[10] But the legacy of the butter-and-egger also lived on as an architectural detail outside the new Merc building: the seventeen-story edifice featured a frieze depicting farm animals and bountiful baskets of eggs.

The "Big Butter and Egg Man"

In his heyday, the butter-and-egg man became a key figure in the cultural lexicon. The butter-and-egg man, initially, was a name for the merchants who sold either or both of the dairy products. At his most successful, the butter-and-egg man operated a warehouse or perhaps a storefront in the city, like the old-guard butter-and-eggers who once sold and stored dairy products in warehouses around what is now New York's Tribeca neighborhood. Later on, the phrase was meant to refer to the gentlemen who speculated in such commodities on the exchange floor.

prices. Most notably, in 1996, Kraft Foods was accused of reducing the price of bulk cheese and milk through trading activity on the NCE. Although the resulting class-action lawsuits were ultimately dismissed, the Green Bay exchange was closed, and all trading moved to the CME in 1997.*

Less than 1 percent of the cheese manufactured in the United States is traded at the CME, even though the vast majority of buyers and sellers continue to look to the exchange to determine their prices, particularly around the Super Bowl, the largest cheese-buying event of the year.

Why trade cheddar in particular? Because it accounts for 35 percent of U.S. cheese production and is a multibillion-dollar industry. That said, according to USDA statistics, varieties other than American cheeses, mostly Italian, now have a combined level of production that easily exceeds American cheeses. Could mozzarella or Parmesan futures be on the horizon?

*Dave Newbart, "Cheese Is a New Slice of Business for the Merc," *Chicago Tribune*, May 2, 1997.

George S. Kaufman's play *Butter and Egg Man*—about a midwestern sucker so free with his money that some eastern city slickers take him for a ride—opened on Broadway in 1925, and then played out on stages across the country. In 1928, the comedy was released as a silent film, to tepid acclaim. In 1926, Louis Armstrong recorded a hit song called "Big Butter and Egg Man." Although the song is more notable as an infectious jazz track rather than for the lyrics (essentially, about a woman looking for a free-spending butter-and-egg man to take her out on the town), it no doubt further popularized the term. After that, butter-and-egg men were often mentioned in the society and humor pages—in the same sentence as "chorus girls." The name is clearly meant to disparage: the butter-and-egger was seen as nouveau riche, a philanderer with a taste for naive bottle-blondes, and frequently something of a dupe.

A handful of hardworking real-life butter-and-egg men apparently took offense at the disparaging implication that all those in the profession were ostentatious spendthrifts; one Minneapolis butter-and-egg dealer went so far as to sue the vaudeville theater that staged *Butter and Egg Man*.

The $100,000 complaint was filed against the Minneapolis theater and its star, actress Frankie Heath, charging that when the actress sang the song "Butter and Eggs," she used "certain tones and gestures to convey that all dealers in butter and eggs were men of immoral and licentious character . . . and thereby hold[s] plaintiff and others similarly situated to hatred, contempt and ridicule." Hooted the newspaper headline: "Butter and Egg Men Hard B'iled."[11]

The Slow Demise of Egg Trading

During World War II, government-imposed price controls nearly snuffed out commodities trading altogether. Further, advances made as a function of the war diminished the need for an egg futures contract. The ability to roof chicken coops with aluminum helped maintain even temperatures inside the buildings year round. As a result, chickens began laying eggs all twelve months of the year rather than just in March, April, and May, and the seasonal need to hedge eggs vanished.[12] Egg production had surged to such a degree that one Chicago poultry representative was prompted to exaggerate that the industry had eggs "virtually running out of our ears."[13]

While the advent of mechanical refrigeration cooled volatile pricing, consumption rose, and markets became more complex as dairy products were available year round. By 1950, eggs had ceased to need a futures market, and over the next couple of decades, egg trading developed a dastardly reputation, prone to corners and squeezes. A later Merc chairman, Leo Melamed, quipped, "I used to say three housewives could get together on the weekend and corner the egg market."[14]

Like many commodities, interest in egg trading eventually dwindled, and by the 1960s, the Merc had diversified, trading hogs, hams, turkeys, pork bellies, and Idaho potatoes. Eggs became less important, and the egg contract was revised to reflect the changing times. Limited to fresh eggs, the new contract, with its realistic value, allowed for better futures forecasting. In 1945, an estimated 50 percent of all storage eggs found their way onto the retail market. By 1968, there were approximately 500,000 cases of eggs produced in one day, and they were on the market within twenty-four hours. Modern production had become a year-round business. Producers, processors, and users had a better guide for price insurance through hedging.[15]

In 1969 and 1970, a number of class-action lawsuits were filed related to egg contracts. One was brought against an East Coast egg distributor, another by a group of futures speculators who claimed the CME had manipulated shell egg futures contracts. Though eggs weren't the Merc's most actively traded commodity, the contracts had become a source of allegations against various traders and commercial interests that were accused of manipulating prices in violation of the Sherman Antitrust Act. The wave of suits kept the Merc's Internal Audit and Investigations Department on its toes. In 1970, the Commodity Exchange Authority, then the futures exchanges watchdog, concluded that the spot markets in eggs on both the New York Mercantile Exchange and the CME had "outlived their usefulness."[16]

The contract for frozen eggs, introduced in 1949, also hit the skids in the 1970s, as users, such as bakers, candy makers, and mayonnaise processors, switched to liquid eggs, which had the advantage of no storage charges or time lost to thawing. However, eggs were fast becoming a vestige of the past—the future, many exchanges decided, was in financial instruments.

Then again, eggs weren't dead yet: in the mid-1970s, they were temporarily revitalized, thanks to a small change: the egg contract now called for delivery of a certificate, rather than the eggs themselves. Traders, it was believed, would be less hesitant to trade paper, while those accepting delivery would find it more convenient to switch delivery locations.[17] Considering the outcry that had taken place in 1917 over "paper eggs," there's considerable irony in the fact that in the 1970s, "paper" trades proved to be the wave of the future, becoming the model for agricultural commodities going forward. Nevertheless, it wasn't enough to save egg trading, which eventually sputtered to a full stop.

What Trades Now

- *Butter*: Trades on the CME. Contract size is 40,000 pounds (18 metric tons). This is grade AA butter.[18]
- *Nonfat Dry Milk*: Trades on the CME. Contract size is 44,000 pounds of grade A and extra grade dry milk. A product of the manufacturing of

butter, nonfat dry milk can be stored, used in various feed and food sources, and/or reconstituted into milk.[19]

- *Milk Class III*: Trades on the CME. Contract size is 200,000 pounds (100 metric tons). Also known as "cheese milk," this milk is used primarily in the manufacture of cheddar cheese.[20]

- *Milk Class IV*: Trades on the CME. Contract size is 200,000 pounds. Used to produce butter and nonfat dry milk.[21]

- *Dry Whey*: Trades on the CME. Contract size is 44,000 pounds. This is a dried form of the liquid that separates from milk during the cheese-making process. Dried whey is used in foods such as crackers, breads and cereal, energy bars, and protein drinks; it is also used in animal feed.[22]

- *Cheese (domestic cheddar)*: Trades on the CME. Contract size is 200,000 pounds for the cash-settled futures contract.[23]

The building to the left with the flag on top is the Tontine Coffee House, which was located at the corner of Wall and Water Streets in New York. During its prime, it was one of the busiest centers for the trading of commodities and stocks. Across Water Street is the Merchant's Coffee House, and to the right is Wall Street. (Walter Monteith Aikman, *The Tontine Coffee House, Wall & Water Streets, About 1797* [1910], engraving after *Tontine Coffee House, N.Y.C.* [ca. 1797], a painting by Francis Guy [New-York Historical Society]; Library of Congress, Prints and Photographs Division)

CHAPTER SIX

The Mochaccino Market

Coffee, Sugar, and Cocoa

Sugar is becoming like gold.

HARRY ADLER, PRESIDENT OF LOCAL BAKING, QUOTED IN
WALL STREET JOURNAL, OCTOBER 16, 1980

I'm not selling for any price at the moment. For us, coffee is like gold.

BRAZILIAN COFFEE FARMER PAULO RIBEIRO, QUOTED
IN *TIME*, JUNE 21, 2005

Cocoa beans, or what [Ghana] locals call "black gold."

WALL STREET JOURNAL, JUNE 27, 2011

There is some symmetry in knowing that much of the earliest trading of coffee (and other commodities) took place in coffeehouses. It is impossible not to make a mental leap to modern-day coffee shops and Starbucks franchises, where many a fledgling business is launched these days. Furthermore, most of the ingredients in the iced double cappuccinos fueling those entrepreneurial pursuits are affected by commodities market trade. Multinational conglomerates, like Nestlé and J. M. Smucker (owner of Folgers Coffee), certainly avail themselves of the commodities exchanges to help buffer against the price swings that can drive up the cost of their key ingredients (and cut into operating profits). Even the tiny niche producers, which are generally outside of the "commodities chain," rely on the benchmarks set through major markets in setting their own asking prices.

"[For] most cups of coffee around the world, we're involved somehow," an official from the IntercontinentalExchange explained to me on condition his name not be used. "We trade arabica coffee, and every bean was probably hedged on the exchange multiple times by the producer waiting for export, the merchant who may have held on to it for two or three years, and the roaster and end user."[1]

East Coast Story

The story of the coffee, sugar, and cocoa markets takes us from Chicago to the East Coast, and to New York in particular. Since none of these commodities were U.S. grown, like grain or corn, all required shipping ports.

As the center of shipping activity, New York thus became the center of trading activity, although coffee exchanges also sprung up in other port cities, notably in Baltimore in 1884 and New Orleans in 1903. However, New York was where most of the action was centered, as exchanges began, splintered, and merged, eventually becoming the New York Board of Trade and, finally, the IntercontinentalExchange. Today, this is the primary U.S. market for coffee, sugar, and cocoa trading.

Coffeehouse Trading

Before any of the lofty exchange buildings and office skyscrapers were constructed, much of the earliest mercantile activity in Europe and America was conducted in coffeehouses, in addition to taverns and other public meeting spaces.

The commodity exchanges had begun in London in the eighteenth century as primitive "rings" or "clubs." These rudimentary groups met in coffeehouses to discuss the prices, shipping possibilities, and other details of trade in tea, tallow, hemp, grain, and of course, coffee. Late-seventeenth-century French traveler Francis Maximilien Misson succinctly summed up the attraction of coffeehouses: "These houses, which are very numerous in London, are extremely convenient. You have all Manner of News there. You have a good fire, which you may sit by as long as you please. You have a Dish of Coffee, you meet your Friends for the Transaction of Business, and all for a penny if you don't care to spend more."[2] Indeed, the early coffeehouse became known as a "penny university" because of the price per cup.

Like the tavern, the coffeehouse was considered a public meeting place for conviviality and company. Also, coffeehouses became important places for the circulation of news and other information. Pamphlets, chapbooks, and other ancestors of today's newspapers were often circulated and discussed at the coffeehouse. Later, when printing became a more established industry, coffeehouses, inhabited by the "chattering classes," provided an environment where the contents of the day's papers were read and the news avidly and loudly discussed. Advertisements for plays and performances, auctions, and other events were often displayed prominently on the walls. Some coffeehouses acted as both reference and lending library, stocking periodicals and books. Many regulars even received their mail at the coffeehouse.

Each coffeehouse specialized in a different type of clientele. Some self-segregated by religious or political beliefs, others by profession. One might attract physicians, another might specialize in literati, lawyers, or merchants. One such establishment, Edward Lloyd's, catered primarily to seafarers and merchants, and Lloyd regularly prepared "ship lists" for underwriters who met there to offer insurance. Thus began Lloyd's of London, the famous insurance company. Other coffeehouses spawned the London Stock Exchange, the Bankers' Clearing-House, and newspapers such as the *Tatler* and the *Spectator*.[3]

What of the coffee itself? According to most accounts, the coffee bore little resemblance to what we drink today, brewed in enormous 8- to 10-gallon pots and served piping hot. It is likely that coffeehouse customers found the brew too bitter, tolerating it only with the addition of milk and sugar as well as other ingredients, such as ale or wine and spices, like clove and cinnamon.[4] With such bad coffee (and access to better and cheaper tea after Britain's conquest of India), perhaps it's little wonder that over the course of the eighteenth century, the British became a tea-drinking culture instead. And in addition to coffee, wine and other beverages were served, lubricating numerous business exchanges.

The coffeehouse tradition extended to the New World as well. This recollection of the Boston Exchange Coffee House in the early nineteenth century sets a typical scene:

> The original purpose in building the Coffee House was to provide appropriate facilities for the "genial institution of Change." This was a

time-honored custom of the merchants to meet on the sidewalk of State Street at about one o'clock as they left their counting-rooms, and talk "shop, ships and politics" for half an hour or so. The whole first story of the ambitious new Coffee House was devoted to a great Exchange Floor.[5]

This was hardly a grubby shop front—no expense was spared for its wealthy clientele, including installation of a "perspective glass" (telescope) to watch for incoming ships and a telegraph to monitor daily news and prices.[6] Gradually, the exchanges became formal institutions, with contracts, rules, and finally, futures trading that made it possible for members to fix prices months into the future.

The Coffee Market

Of the mighty triumvirate that would one day compose the Coffee, Sugar, and Cocoa Exchange (CSCE), the New York Coffee Exchange was established first, in 1882.

While tea played a critical role in the Old World—from both an economic and a culinary standpoint—in the New World, coffee was king. Britain was the hub for importing and trading tea (which has traded briefly on U.S. exchanges), but with the proximity of the United States to coffee-growing countries in Central and South America, coffee played a key role in the early American diet.

Although booze was by far the preferred beverage, throughout the first half of the nineteenth century, the American taste for coffee swelled, particularly after the War of 1812, which temporarily shut off access to tea just when all things French, including coffee drinking, were stylish. By that time, Brazilian coffee was closer and cheaper. Per-capita consumption grew to 3 pounds a year in 1830, 5.5 pounds by 1850, and 8 pounds by 1859. Despite the prevalence of urban coffeehouses, most Americans drank coffee at home or brewed it over campfires while heading west.[7]

Prior to the Civil War, New Orleans had been the major point of entry for coffee in the United States. A war blockade closed the port, however, and New York subsequently became the hub of the American coffee trade.[8] Europeans drank (and traded in) coffee, of course. But by the 1870s, coffee had become downright indispensable to Americans, who consumed six times as much as most Europeans. By 1876, the United States was importing 340 million pounds of coffee annually, accounting for nearly one-third of all coffee exported from producing countries.[9] Coffee had become big business in America, and businessmen needed to find a way to protect their interests.

The coffee market has always been volatile. Rumors of Brazilian frosts cause price hikes, while large harvests produce sharp declines. Since coffee trees take four or five years to mature, that diminishes near-term harvest predictability. Unlike wheat or corn, coffee grows on a perennial plant, and a coffee farm involves a major commitment of capital that cannot easily be switched to another crop. And all of this is complicated by the effects of plant disease, war, political upheaval, and market manipulation. Although a volatile market means increased risk, it also means increased opportunities for speculators to trade and potentially profit. As the coffee industry boomed during the 1870s, large importing firms made huge profits but at substantial risk. The story of how the first U.S. coffee exchange came to be begins with three firms known as the Trinity: B. G. Arnold (also called the "Napoleon of the Coffee Trade"), Bowie Dash, and O. G. Kimball. They were the leaders in the coffee importing (and speculating) business, and those benefiting from the Trinity's success enjoyed a comfortable New York life.

When it became clear, in 1878, that Brazil was going to flood the market with coffee, the Trinity was unable to demand favorable prices. On December 4, 1880, O. G. Kimball died in Boston. Only forty-two, Kimball had no known health problems; some speculated that his death was a "coffee suicide." Regardless of the actual cause, his death practically dissolved his firm, causing considerable uneasiness among creditors. The Trinity collapsed like a house of cards. On December 8, the *New York Journal of Commerce* reported that B. G. Arnold had failed. The following day, no one could sell a single bean. Several firms suspended business transactions, and the losses for coffee dealers mounted. "The history of the trade for the twelve months [of 1880] is a record of loss and disaster such as never was experienced before in the coffee trade in the United States," observed Francis Thurber.[10]

Some who had been worst hit by the ruinous 1880 collapse decided to begin a coffee exchange. Modeling itself on the already existing Chicago Board of Trade and the New York Cotton Exchange, the New York Coffee

Exchange was incorporated on December 7, 1881, nearly one year after B. G. Arnold went bankrupt. Benjamin Arnold was one of the incorporators and became the first president.[11]

At first, business was slow and the exchange was a laughingstock, but, eventually, business thrived. Newspapers gleefully reported the escapades of "hilarious coffee brokers." In his 1914 memoir, former commodities broker Abram Wakeman recalls these early days, as silk-hatted young rogues played practical jokes, like dyeing a light-colored pug a dark color to fool a mark or placing phony ads in the newspaper.[12] Similarly, slow days on the Coffee Exchange resulted in bored members diverting themselves with "hat smashing" and launching "wet paper wads" at unsuspecting colleagues and exchange windows.[13] In 1883, an ancillary tea exchange, called the Importers' and Grocers' Exchange, was organized in close proximity to the Coffee Exchange, but it closed in 1885.[14] By century's end, technology had made worldwide communication virtually instantaneous, and coffee exchanges in major European ports corresponded rapidly with colleagues in New York.

The wild gyrations of the coffee market captured the popular imagination too. In 1904, Cyrus Townsend Brady wrote *The Corner in Coffee*, a novel informed by interviews with coffee dealers, brokers, and members of the Coffee Exchange. The overwrought love story, about how the mastermind behind a coffee corner reverses his position to save his girlfriend from losing her fortune, was later staged as a play. In the climactic scene of the book, the hero bears witness to the breaking of his coffee corner:

> The corner was breaking, it was broken!
>
> He tore through the streets like a madman. Across the square, bareheaded in spite of the furious storm, he forced his way through the great crowds until he reached the floor of the Exchange. Around the coffee pit pandemonium reigned. It was the centre, the vortex, of a seething maelstrom of passion. One sale succeeded another, and the market was going down. Down, down, down!
>
> Screaming men were frantically shaking their nervous hands aloft before Drewitt, the junior partner of Cutter, Drewitt & Co., who was selling as imperturbably as he had bought. The Exchange was in a perfect roar. . . . Clothes were torn, a man fell and was trampled by the

maddened crowd. . . . Coffee fell twenty cents a pound in two hours. . . . The bears had won.[15]

Sugar Joins the Coffee Exchange

Like coffee, sugar played a key role in mercantile history. Sugar along with tobacco and tea, posits historian Sidney W. Mintz, "were the first objects within capitalism that conveyed with their use the complex idea that one could *become* different by *consuming* differently."[16] But unlike coffee, sugar had a wider range of utility. Of course, it served as both sweetener and confection—the latter especially valued as dessert became a course unto itself on dinner tables in the late nineteenth century. But as the availability of sugar spread from the very rich to the masses, it became clear that its value also lay in its caloric contribution and its use as a preservative, extending the life of perishable fruit in marmalade and jams, syrups, candied fruits, and other preserves. And of course, sugar could be distilled into rum, a favorite tipple in both England and the new American colonies.

Like the coffeehouses of England, sugar too was exported from the old world to the new. On his second voyage to the New World, Christopher Columbus brought sugarcane from the Canary Islands. Sugar planting began in earnest in the sixteenth century in Hispaniola (the area that now includes the Dominican Republic and Haiti), and by 1546, according to the colony's official historian, Gonzalo Fernández de Oviedo y Valdés, Hispaniola boasted twenty "powerful mills and four horse mills, and . . . ships come from Spain continuously and return with cargoes of sugar and the skimmings and molasses that are lost would make a great province rich."[17]

However, Cuba soon rose to become the center of the sugar industry. During the Seven Years' War, Britain had briefly occupied Cuba and jump-started the island's sugar production. A giant market for Cuban sugar opened up during the American Revolution when Britain banned exports from her sugar colonies to rebellious American colonists. As Cuban planters stepped in, "sugar fever" seized the island. The collapse of Haiti's sugar industry further propelled Cuba's rise to sugar greatness.

Louisiana was the distant-second supplier of sugar to the American people, as planters and sugar experts fleeing the Haitian revolution transformed the area into a sugar economy. By 1812, when Louisiana joined the United States as a slave state, it had seventy-five sugar mills.[18] But Louisiana growers were plagued by a very short growing season, the possibility of frost, and drought in the summer. Further, the Civil War brought Louisiana's sugar industry to a near halt. "The sugar plantations had been abandoned, neglected or laid waste and plundered by Union troops," recounts Elizabeth Abbott in her history of sugar. "From 1861 to 1864, the number of Louisiana's working sugar plantations had been reduced from 1,200 to 231, and sugar production had plunged from roughly 264,000 tons to a mere 6,000."[19] Even fifteen years after the war, more than between two in three sugar plantations remained closed.

With Cuba's position as the chief supplier of sugar solidified, American capital gravitated to the island nation. By 1896, direct American investment in Cuba, including sugar, cattle ranching, tobacco estates, and fruit, was an estimated $950 million. This involved the nineteen Cuban refineries owned by the American Sugar Refining Company, or the Sugar Trust, formed in 1888, representing the consolidation of twenty-one refining companies in seven cities. The Sugar Trust refined 70 to 90 percent of America's sugar.[20] According to some estimates, by 1907, the Sugar Trust owned or controlled a whopping 98 percent of the sugar-processing capacity in the United States.

Meanwhile, exchanges trading cane sugar and beet sugar futures operated in London and Hamburg—and had done so since the 1890s. (Beet sugar, considered to be of higher quality, was the preferred sweetener in Europe. Also, it is worth noting that in the late nineteenth and early twentieth centuries, sugar beets were planted in the northern United States and Canada for consumption by Americans.) But in response to World War I closing down the European sugar exchanges, the Coffee Exchange expanded its facilities to include sugar in December 1914 and changed its name in late 1916, establishing the New York Coffee and Sugar Exchange.[21] Many were delighted to see the balance of power shift away from the strict control exerted by the Sugar Trust monopoly, which was dissolved by the government. "Sugar has become far too important an article to permit of its control by one particular interest," declared the New York Coffee and Sugar Exchange in 1924.[22]

Today, Brazil is the world's largest sugarcane producer and exporter, and of all the sugar produced now, about 75 percent is from cane sugar and only 25 percent from beet sugar.[23] This is significant for two reasons: First, sugarcane is a perennial plant, while the sugar beet is an annual. Because of its longer production cycle, sugarcane is less influenced by changes in price. And second, about half of Brazilian sugar is transformed into ethanol.

Cane blackstrap molasses also had a brief turn on the trading floor, with futures trading inaugurated in 1931. By 1952, when the New York Coffee and Sugar Exchange celebrated its seventy-year anniversary by publishing a commemorative book on its history and operations, trading in this commodity had already become "negligible" and presumably halted shortly thereafter. During World War I, molasses "became of great importance in the manufacture of munitions," and "assumed even greater importance in World War II in the manufacture of alcohol for explosives and synthetic rubber."[24] But in peacetime, blackstrap molasses was better suited to baking and the manufacturing of rum.

Cocoa Gets Added to the Mix

As the New York Coffee and Sugar Exchange gained steam, it wasn't until later that a need for trading in cocoa was established. The New York Cocoa Exchange was created in 1925 as an "adjunct" to the New York Coffee and Sugar Exchange. In January 1926, the name was changed briefly to the Cocoa and Rubber Exchange of America. Six months later, it was switched back to the New York Cocoa Exchange. The exchange immediately became the preeminent marketplace for setting cocoa prices; within three years, trading volume outpaced the combined volume of the two next-largest cocoa exchanges—London and Liverpool. Two-thirds of the cocoa traded was produced in West Africa; other cocoa-production countries included Brazil, Ceylon, Costa Rica, Java, Trinidad, and Venezuela.[25]

Compared with midwestern marts, where many of the traders had their roots in the farming or processing industries and remembered the feel of the grain or the smell of the stockyards, in 1930s New York, a generation of traders speculated on foodstuffs grown on faraway shores, without ever setting foot in commodities production.

As a common household provision, coffee was a known quantity—but cocoa arrived in processed form, usually as a powder or chocolate confection. So great was the divide, that at the Cocoa Exchange's tenth anniversary celebration, held at the Waldorf Astoria hotel, the evening's

CORNERING THE CHOCOLATE MARKET

One of the most fascinating modern-day tales of cornering the market is that of British hedge fund manager Anthony Ward. Labeled "ChocFinger" and "Willy Wonka" in the tabloids, Ward all but cornered the market in cocoa in 2010. Through his private investment firm, Armajaro, Ward snapped up 240,000 tons of chocolate, or 7 percent of global production—enough, according to one estimate, to make more than 5 billion chocolate bars. It wasn't his first time, either; in 2002, he had purchased 150,000 tons of cocoa, or around 5 percent of global production.*

Perhaps even more amazingly, in an age when many traders never see the physical commodities they trade, Ward actually took delivery of the beans himself, secreting them away throughout Europe. "The beans now lie refrigerated in warehouses in undisclosed locations across Europe," the *Economist* reported. "They can stay there for up to 20 years, although Armajaro hopes to have taken profits long before that."†

decor included a backdrop of palm trees and a pyramid of 30,000 pounds of cocoa beans behind the dais. "The Exchange is attempting to acquaint commodity traders with the actual raw cocoa bean from which finished chocolate is manufactured."[26] Some might say this was a sign of things to come—a foreshadowing of current trading dynamics in which speculators go an entire career trading "paper" commodities, never setting foot on a farm or seeing a hill of cocoa beans.

The Cocoa Exchange would continue to operate separately for several decades. Even as the New York Coffee and Sugar Exchange joined the New York Produce Exchange and others on the modern trading floor of the brand-new Commodity Exchange Center at the World Trade Center in 1977, the Cocoa Exchange was one of the few excluded. While the other exchanges moved into the electronic age, the Cocoa Exchange languished in its obsolete facilities, which resulted in snarled trading and market shutdowns on unusually busy days. Meanwhile, the center of cocoa trading had moved from New York to London, where volume generally ran double the New York level. Indeed, when London trading ceased for the day around noon eastern time, activity on the New York Cocoa Exchange often ground

As a result of Ward's 2010 activity, cocoa organizations complained to London's financial regulators. It was the largest delivery of cocoa on the London exchange in at least a decade, and Ward became the go-to source for chocolate manufacturers looking for beans. Other investors cried foul, claiming that Ward was driving up prices on a commodity that had already increased in value by more than 150 percent over the previous two and a half years.

The financial media still covers ChocFinger's every move with ardent interest, especially when the cocoa market surges or falls. In any case, chocolate lovers should not worry too much, analysts say. Cocoa accounts for only about 10 percent of the price of most ordinary chocolate bars.

*Julia Werdigier and Julie Creswell, "Trader's Cocoa Binge Wraps Up Chocolate Market," *New York Times*, July 24, 2010.

†"Sweet Dreams: A Hedge Fund Bets Big on Chocolate," *Economist*, August 5, 2010.

to a halt. Snarked a *Wall Street Journal* reporter: "On the New York Cocoa Exchange these days, business is about as lackluster as the faint gray tiles that cover the walls and floor of the trading room. Bored futures traders sit by their telephones reading, waiting for something to do."[27]

Few were surprised when the New York Cocoa Exchanged merged into the New York Coffee and Sugar Exchange on September 28, 1979, creating the Coffee, Sugar, and Cocoa Exchange (CSCE). In 1998, the New York Board of Trade became the parent company for both the New York Cotton Exchange (which also included orange juice contracts) and the Coffee, Sugar, and Cocoa Exchange. And on September 14, 2006, the IntercontinentalExchange (ICE) agreed to become the parent company of the NYBOT, a transaction completed on January 12, 2007.

What Trades Now

• *Cocoa*: Trades on the ICE. Contract size is 22,000 pounds (10 metric tons). This is the benchmark for global cocoa prices. Key cocoa products

THE HERSHEY BAR INDEX

A nonscientific but highly entertaining measure of the value of cocoa and sugar is the Hershey Bar Index. Compiled by Lynne Olver of the Food Timeline Web site, with price and weight data provided by the Hershey Company, the index tracks the evolution of the famous Hershey bar from 1908 to 1986. It is fascinating to see how even during Hershey's "nickel bar" years, the company accordingly trimmed or padded the candy bar based on the going rate of commodity prices.

[1908] 9⁄16 oz.....2 cents	[1941] 1¼ oz.....5 cents
[1918] 16⁄16 oz.....3 cents	[1944] 1⅝ oz.....5 cents
[1920] 9⁄16 oz.....3 cents	[1946] 1½ oz.....5 cents
[1921] 1 oz.....5 cents	[1947] 1 oz.....5 cents
[1924] 1⅜ oz.....5 cents	[1954] ⅞ oz.....5 cents
[1930] 2 oz.....5 cents	[1955] 1 oz.....5 cents
[1933] 1⅝ oz.....5 cents	[1958] ⅞ oz.....5 cents
[1936] 1½ oz.....5 cents	[1960] 1 oz.....5 cents
[1937] 1⅝ oz.....5 cents	[1963] ⅞ oz.....5 cents
[1938] 1⅜ oz.....5 cents	[1965] 1 oz.....5 cents
[1939] 1⅝ oz.....5 cents	[1966] ⅞ oz.....5 cents

include cocoa liquor, cocoa butter, cocoa cake, and cocoa powder. The chocolate market is the largest user of cocoa, but products like cocoa butter can be used in a variety of nonfood products, such as soap and cosmetics.[28]

• *Coffee C*: Trades on the ICE. Contract size is 37,500 pounds (17 metric tons). This is the world benchmark for arabica coffee.[29]

• *Robusta*: Trades on the ICE. Contract size is 37,500 pounds. Robusta is less precious than arabica coffee but accounts for more than 40 percent of the world's coffee production and one-third of the world's coffee exports.[30]

• *Sugar No. 11*: Trades on the ICE. Contract size is 112,000 pounds (50 metric tons).[31] This is the benchmark for global raw cane sugar and trades

[1968] ¾ oz.....5 cents	[1978] 1.2 oz.....25 cents
[1969] 1½ oz.....10 cents	[1980] 1.05 oz.....25 cents
[1970] 1⅜ oz.....10 cents	[1982] 1.45 oz.....30 cents
[1973] 1.26 oz......10 cents	[1983] 1.45 oz.....35 cents
[1974] 1.4 oz.....15 cents	[1986] 1.45 oz.....40 cents
[1976] 1.2 oz.....15 cents	[1986] 1.65 oz.....40 cents
[1977] 1.2 oz......20 cents	

Olver added some occasional price points after 1986. With the weight of the Hershey bar stabilized at about 1.55 ounces, she observed the following prices at various retail outlets:

[1991] 45 cents
[1995] 50 cents
[2007] 79 cents
[2008] 59 cents
[2009] $1.10
[2010] 95 cents

Lynne Olver, "The Hershey Bar Index," The Food Timeline, http://www.foodtimeline.org/foodfaq5.html#candybar (accessed November 3, 2011). Reprinted with kind permission of Lynne Olver.

actively—in 2010, Sugar No. 11 had the third-highest trading volume, behind only corn and soybeans, among food-based contracts in the United States.[32] According to a representative from the ICE, Sugar No. 11 is "world sugar," which is "generally grown and delivered out of the USA."[33]

• *Sugar No. 16*: Trades on the ICE. Contract size is 112,000 pounds.[34] This contract, like the others, represents raw cane sugar. It began trading in 2008. According to a representative from the ICE, Sugar No 16 is "domestic sugar," which is "generally produced and delivered in the USA; this is the market that is protected by import quotas."[35] This contract serves the hedging needs of U.S. sugar producers, end users, and merchants.

A buyer inspects cattle at the vast Union Stockyards in Chicago (1941), with signs for meatpacking giants Armour and Swift in the background. (Library of Congress, Prints and Photographs Division)

CHAPTER SEVEN

Cattle Call

Despite the rancher's romance of owning a herd,
profit is no longer in ownership, but in trading.

BETTY FUSSELL,
RAISING STEAKS: THE LIFE AND TIMES OF AMERICAN BEEF

A number of animal proteins have been traded on the commodities market, and nearly all have come and gone. Eggs had their heyday, of course; turkey futures and "broilers" (chickens) had their stint; shrimp had a short-lived run in the United States, though it continues to trade on certain Asian exchanges; and even pork belly futures have come and gone. Meanwhile, beef futures have solidly stood the test of time.

There's a reason modern-day money words such as "pecuniary," "capital," and "bull market" all have their linguistic roots in . . . cattle. Some money words harken back to the Latin or Middle English for "cattle." The Latin word for "money," *pecunia*, comes from *pecus* (cattle). Interestingly, Roman coins were often stamped with the figure of a bull; the English word "capital" comes from the Anglo-French *chattel* (cattle). The "bull market," so dear to traders and analysts, comes from the potential of breeding more cattle.

Ranchers have long associated cattle with money. The dairy cows might as well exude the jingle of coins with their milk, while the freeloading beef cattle (or "beeves," for short) become moneymakers only after slaughter. Of course, the Chicago Merc was born from butter and eggs, evolving by the late 1920s into a meaty livestock-oriented exchange, trading cattle, hogs and pork bellies, "fresh broilers" (slaughtered chickens), and eggs. Across town, the Chicago Board of Trade (CBOT) did a hearty business in grains—wheat and corn, as well as soybeans, oats, rye, and barley, in addition to cotton.

Although nothing seems as American now as juicy hamburgers and sizzling steaks, cattle were not indigenous to the New World. According to historian Betty Fussell, Columbus brought the first cattle to Hispaniola in 1493, both for food and to assist the settlers in their work. But the Dutch West India Company delivered the first cattle to North America through the Dutch colonial settlement of New Amsterdam (now New York City) in 1625. The settlers brought "three heifers and a bull." Within five years, the company inventoried sixty cows and forty-seven horses, but grain shortages from failing wheat crops diminished the herds, and new boatloads of cattle had to be sent from Holland. The small stream—called *de wal*—that the Dutch had built along the palisades across the lower part of the island to keep the natives out was dubbed Bloody Run during the winter slaughtering season, when as many as four thousand cattle were slaughtered on its banks. Eventually, such facilities became so numerous and so odoriferous that they were ordered to move to a public facility created for them on Pearl Street, to the north of *de wal*, or Wall Street.[1]

The Early Cattle Trade in New York

At first, the cattle trade was big business in New York, apparently creating quite the bustle and stench. One 1848 article put average weekly sales at an estimated one thousand to twelve hundred head of cattle. It describes the scene in this way: "Monday is the great sale-day on which nearly all the cattle received up to that time are disposed of. . . . The cattle are sold alive, thus paid for and driven off by the purchaser." Disputes related to how the weight of the cattle should be measured were not uncommon, and these disagreements resulted in pricing discrepancies among the New York, Boston, and Philadelphia markets, which would later be cleared up as it became standard practice to telegraph prices to centralized exchanges. The article concludes with a call to remove the slaughterhouses from the city: "The present practice is revolting to the senses and dangerous to the health of our people. We know no other city which aspires to cleanliness or exemption from contagion that tolerates the nuisance."[2]

By the 1850s, another tally shows that for the full year 1853, 157,420 beeves and 10,720 cows and calves were sold. Again, these were sales of live animals, not "dressed" cattle.[3]

Ranchers were expanding westward, and most of their cattle came from east of the Mississippi: Indiana, Kentucky, and Tennessee were considered the greatest contributors. Thanks to the burgeoning railroads, "for every hundred that come to us on foot, a thousand reach us by the speedier transit afforded by railroad, and whatever may be the immediate excess of expense which the latter may involve, we think it is more than made up by a saving of time, and the fresher, and therefore the more marketable condition of the cattle when they are brought to the city." Market days had expanded from just Monday to both Monday and Thursday; most of the live cattle sales took place in what is now midtown Manhattan (one market, on Forty-fourth Street and Fifth Avenue, and two more, on Sixty-sixth Street; the fourth market held at "the lower of Hudson River Bull's Head").[4]

British Beef Eaters

England's role in the development of America's beef trade is considerable. As "the great beef-eaters of Europe," the English (at least the middle and upper classes) consumed far more beef than their continental neighbors. Meat, and particularly beef, was believed to ensure greater strength and virility. It wasn't just part of the meal, beef was part of the lifestyle, conveying affluence and contentment. In the late 1700s, "livestock portraits became a favorite among Englishmen of the period. Many a country estate and English drawing room boasted paintings of obese cattle in the foreground of a bucolic landscape."[5] And as America built up through the 1800s, and an anthrax epidemic on the European continent spread to Ireland and England in the 1860s, making British beef scarce and expensive, the British turned to the Americas to supply them with additional beef. Live cattle and salted beef were shipped across the Atlantic, in steadily increasing amounts.

As America pushed westward, grazing cattle on the fertile and abundant grasses of the Midwest, the big question was how to connect those fields with consumers in the East, as well as with those famished English overseas. The answer came in the 1870s with the westward expansion of the American railroads. British companies played a major role in financing the building of those transcontinental railroads in the 1870s and 1880s, and "moving cattle by rail from west to east became a primary commercial objective of the new British-financed railroads," writes historian Jeremy Rifkin.[6] British and Scottish financiers began to catch cattle fever. "In Edinburgh, the ranch pot was boiling over," recounts John Clay, an agent for English investors, in his 1924 autobiography. "Drawing rooms buzzed with the stories of this last of bonanzas; staid old gentlemen, who scarcely knew the difference between a steer and a heifer, discussed it over their port and nuts."[7]

But the biggest excitement of all for the British beef eaters was the advent of refrigerated compartments. The cost of shipping live animals to Europe (in terms of special shipping decks, damage to animals, weight losses) encouraged innovations in transporting dressed meats. Young New York inventor John I. Bates experimented with hanging beef carcasses in rooms loaded with ice and circulating the cold air with large fans. In June 1875, he shipped ten carcasses to England. They arrived fresh and sparked a flurry of interest among British investors. Timothy Eastman, a successful packer, bought Bates's patent and launched an ambitious campaign to ship refrigerated carcasses to Britain. By the end of the year, Eastman transported more than 206,000 pounds of beef; by the following year, he began shipping a million pounds of beef per month. By the close of that year, the Eastman operation was providing the British Isles with 3 million pounds of fresh beef every month. Other companies followed Eastman's lead. Soon, nearly every steamer that set off from New York or Philadelphia to England carried American beef.[8] By the late nineteenth century, America was responsible for 90 percent of the beef imported to England.[9]

The advent of refrigerated train cars in the 1870s also meant that cattle could be slaughtered close to the farm and then the butchered meat could be transported, eliminating the need to ship live cattle to market. This had enormous implications for the farmers and meat packers. As Fussell summarizes, "This was the first major step in separating the producers and packinghouse/processors of meat from the eaters of it." By 1884, the number of cattle slaughtered in Chicago was so significant, the phrase "meatpacking" replaced "pork packing" as the name of the industry.

With refrigeration solving the biggest beef transport issue, British and Scottish bankers and "armchair cowboys" began piling on, forming the Anglo-American Cattle Company, the Colorado Mortgage and Investment Company of London, and the Prairie Cattle Company (chaired by the

Earl of Arlee), to name just a few, all eagerly snapping up land and cattle. Some English lords even built their own "castles on the prairie," expensive estates adorned with the best English furnishings and stocked with the finest European wines and delicacies; they even boasted a full complement of servants and livery. Many of these prairie ranch homes served as summer retreats or vacation houses for the British ruling class, who entertained friends with hunting trips and wilderness excursions.[10] As a result, anti-British sentiment soon ran high. In the summer of 1884, both the Democratic and Republican conventions included planks in their campaign platforms calling for curbs on "alien holdings" in the United States.

But the British brought with them more than just their capital. They brought their unique taste for "fatted" beef. The British consumer insisted on heavy beef, richly marbled with speckles of fat. And the new British cattle barons had a strategy for achieving this fatty beef: for the first time in agricultural history, they brought together cattle production and grain production into a new symbiotic relationship.[11] (To this day, it is common to hedge cattle and corn futures together.) In particular, the farmers and businessmen hit on the idea of shipping Indiana cattle into the state to be fed a rich diet of corn before being taken to the slaughterhouses in Cincinnati. The corn followed the cows west, and it soon became common practice to ship cattle from the prairies, where they grazed on grass most of their lives, to be fattened, or "finished," on corn before being sent to St. Louis or Chicago for slaughter. By the 1870s, the Midwest was awash in corn; the crop was so abundant that farmers increased their demand for feeder cattle from the Great Plains (chapter 3).[12] After 1900, the yearly fluctuation in cattle production and consumer demand for beef began to seriously affect the price of corn.[13] The two markets were now firmly intertwined.

Slowly, Americans adopted the British taste for fatty beef—there was no other choice. Furthermore, in 1927, the USDA codified fatty beef as the standard for judging the value and price of beef sold to American consumers.[14] Even today, degree and distribution of marbling is the primary determinant of quality grade: "prime," the highest quality, signifies abundant marbling; "choice" indicates a moderate amount of marbling; and "select" lets consumers know the beef is practically devoid of marbling.[15]

Cattle trade took off in the mid-nineteenth century, as the confluence of commodity brokers, the railroad, and the telegraph meant that even isolated farmers and ranchers could achieve national distribution of their products and so could rise up from subsistence living.

Cattle Trade Moves West

Once again, geography would prove to be destiny for the American settler. While the fertile area that would become the Midwest proved remarkable for growing grain, corn, and other crops, the arid lands of the High Plains proved more precarious for crop growth. This area included what would become southeastern Wyoming, southwestern South Dakota, western Nebraska, eastern Colorado, western Kansas, eastern New Mexico, western Oklahoma, and northwestern Texas. It provided fine grazing land for livestock. Traveling west even now, it is impossible not to notice that farms give way to vast ranches.

In a mere twenty years, from 1867 to 1887, the shift from a rural (small-farm) economy to a giant urban industrial one was "tectonic," Fussell says. "Urban livestock markets shifted from the East to the Midwest, intensifying in turn the shift from the mixed farming of the East to large-scale ranching in the West as settlers, entrepreneurs, and engineers moved ever westward, gobbling up land."[16] Between 1867 and 1880, four major railroads crossed the plains: the Union Pacific, Kansas Pacific, Northern Pacific, and the Santa Fe.

Cattle grew increasingly important in terms of food as the indigenous buffalo (or bison) that once "blackened the prairies" quickly disappeared during the railroad's westward push. As William Cronon writes, "With the arrival of the Union Pacific in Nebraska and Wyoming during the 1860s, followed a few years later by the Kansas Pacific farther south, the railroads drove a knife into the heart of buffalo country."[17] However, this was in many ways a self-perpetuating cycle: to gain land on which to build the railroads and graze cattle, it was deemed necessary to push out the Native Americans who lived on the land, and exterminating their primary food source—the buffalo—was considered a prime means to that end. With the buffalo gone, cattle assumed greater importance as a food supply.

Even before the bison had completely disappeared, cattle began to make buffalo country their own. In the years after its battle with Mexico for independence, Texas was home to myriad wild cattle. The area had indeed proved to be an ideal breeding ground for the bovines, with its mild climate and plentiful grass and water. But when Spanish ranchers fled south of the Rio Grande, they abandoned their herds to the wild. In 1836, the new Republic of Texas declared the feral cattle to be part of the public domain, and young "cowboys" began rounding up, corralling, and driving the wild cattle to stock pens. The Civil War added to the surplus, as it cut off the ranchers of South Texas from their ordinary markets in the Caribbean islands and the slave states of the southern Mississippi Valley. The cattle population grew dramatically during the war years, and by the time the South surrendered, millions of Texas longhorns wandered freely in the region east and south of San Antonio, setting the stage for the great cattle drives of the 1860s through 1880s.[18]

But the point of these iconic cattle drives was to get the livestock to the Midwest, where they could be more easily shipped by rail to supply demand on the East Coast. In the early years, it was challenging to connect the surplus of Texas cattle with the eastern railroads, which were just extending their rails to the outskirts of the western prairies. In 1867, Joseph McCoy, a young entrepreneur, hit on the idea of building a link. He successfully lobbied the governor of Kansas to lift the quarantine on Texas cattle entering the state (Texas fever, a serious cattle disease spread by ticks, had recently decimated the livestock industry) as well as the Illinois legislature to amend its law to allow shipments of cattle into that state. Thus began the reinvigoration of the old Chisholm Trail, which ran cattle from Texas to the railroad in Abilene, Kansas (it had started its life as "a very small, dead place, consisting of about one dozen log huts"[19]). Cowboys would drive the herd, covering ten to twelve miles a day on the three-month trek north to the rail link. The trick was to drive them slowly, pasturing the cattle along the way, as fast-moving animals quickly lost weight. On September 5, 1867, McCoy shipped twenty railroad cars of cattle east from Abilene. By 1871, Abilene was processing 700,000 longhorn steers annually, all bound east for the abattoirs of St. Louis and Chicago.[20]

The Beef Trust

In the years following the Civil War, the "American cattle complex" evolved into a corporate structure. Fed by cattle from the South and Midwest

THE CLINTONS AND CATTLE FUTURES

In 1994, Hillary Rodham Clinton was first lady of the United States. Just as congressional hearings were getting under way for the Whitewater controversy, an uproar broke out over her decades-earlier dealings in cattle futures. During the late 1970s, when she was the first lady of Arkansas and cattle prices were skyrocketing, Clinton opened a trading account at Refco, a New York–based financial services company, with a $1,000 check. Over a nine-month stint and with no prior trading experience, she parlayed her initial investment into a profit of nearly $100,000. Almost two decades later, when this incident came to light, experts wondered aloud how this could possibly be. Quipped Mark Powers, then editor of the *Journal of Futures Markets*, "This is like buying ice skates one day and entering the Olympics a day later."*

How did Clinton get tangled up in cattle futures, many wondered? Jim Blair, an attorney and friend of the Clintons, had encouraged Hillary to speculate in the Chicago futures markets. And he had one of the sharpest

prairies, a new generation of businessmen and entrepreneurs moved quickly to wield its power over the slaughterhouses, rail routes, and distribution outlets. Just as Cincinnati became "Porkopolis," designed to speed hogs into pork, Chicago had its mighty Beef Trust, centered first and foremost in Chicago, but also in the meat-processing cities of St. Louis, Cincinnati, and Kansas City. In 1867, Armour Meat Packers opened its first plant at the Union Stock Yards in Chicago. Eventually, making up the Beef Trust were the Big Five slaughter-packers known as Armour, Cudahy, Hammond, Morris, and Swift. Within a twenty-year period, Chicago came to control 50 percent of the cattle market in America, and by 1900, it had increased its control to 90 percent, with the trust fixing prices at both ends—for producers and consumers. At the same time, the cattle population in America more than doubled, from 15 million in 1870 to 35 million in 1900.[21] On the eve of World War I, the five companies controlled more than two-thirds of the country's beef output and half of its total red meat production. It was found that in violation of federal law, the Beef Trust companies conspired to fix prices and control markets. After the United States Supreme Court issued an injunction against the trust in 1903, three of the five companies—Armour, Morris, and Swift—created a new entity brokers anywhere—Robert L. (Red) Bone, who managed Refco and was a former World Series of Poker semifinalist. Further, it came to light that Bone and Refco were under investigation by the Chicago Mercantile Exchange for systematic violations of Merc rules during the entire period Clinton was their client, culminating in a three-year suspension for Bone.

Despite rampant speculation in the media, ultimately, the issue was swept under the rug. Leo Melamed at the CME, where the cattle futures were traded, confirmed finding discrepancies in Clinton's trading records. He reported seeing no explicit evidence of any wrongdoing. "Mrs. Clinton violated no rules in the course of her transactions," he said at the time. Clinton was never investigated or charged. The incident had little effect on market activity and no influence on food pricing or supply, but it brought the cattle futures market to greater public awareness for a time.

*Quoted in Mark Hosenball and Eleanor Clift, "Hillary's Adventures in Cattle Futures Land," *Newsweek*, April 10, 1994.

called the National Packing Company, which began purchasing its competitors and related businesses.[22]

Also, the Beef Trust was a notable target in Upton Sinclair's book *The Jungle*, in which he wrote about deplorable conditions in "Packingtown" and rampant corruption in the meatpacking industry: "It seemed that they must have agencies all over the country, to hunt out old and crippled and diseased cattle to be canned. There were cattle which had been fed on 'whiskey-malt,' the refuse of the breweries, and had become what the men called 'steerly'—which means covered with boils."[23] First published in serial form in 1905, Sinclair's graphic treatise of how meat products were manufactured had an important influence on the subsequent passage of the Federal Meat Inspection Act and the Pure Food and Drug Act, both enacted in 1906.

Trading "On the Hoof"

There is no doubt that the 1860s were a key time for the cattle industry's migration to Chicago. One century later, another seminal event happened

BEEF'S BULL RUN

In 2011, U.S. live cattle prices rose 13 percent,* making cattle among the few widely traded commodities besides gold to log a double-digit gain. And that was on top of a 26 percent jump in 2010. Retail beef prices rose at supermarkets during the same period, though the trajectory has been gentler than that seen in commodities marts; beef steak prices showed a 14 percent increase from 2009 to 2011, and beef roasts rose 15 percent in the same time frame. What's behind these rising prices? In addition to stable domestic beef consumption, fast-growing emerging economies are importing ever-greater quantities of U.S. beef as they add more animal protein to their diets. In fact, U.S. beef exports are on track to top by as much as 10 percent the all-time high of 2.5 billion pounds set in 2003, according to the U.S. Department of Agriculture. Apparently, consumers around the world are not having much trouble swallowing steeper beef prices, as sales continue to rise.

*Liam Pleven, "Meat Prices Continue Their Bull Run," *Wall Street Journal*, November 3, 2011.

for the cattle industry, and also in Chicago. On November 30, 1964, the Chicago Merc opened futures contract trading in live cattle—the first time trading on live animals "on the hoof," not a slaughtered foodstuff, had been introduced. Glenn H. Andersen, president of one of Chicago's largest commodity brokerage firms and the broker who brought pork bellies to the Merc (chapter 8), took a trip to Texas and learned about the business.[24]

The market was not without its challenges. Papers were written and symposiums given to noisily debate the viability of trading live animals. First, unlike pork bellies, cattle were alive, which meant greater costs (such as food and transportation) and risk (the death of the cattle before profits were reaped). Some critics argued that the ethics of trading live animals was questionable. Second, most traders believed that to make money, a commodity needed to be seasonal. But the cattle industry didn't have the same seasonal booms and busts; the price changed with production, not with the weather. Third, "grading" is a key component of commodities—it is important that the product, whether corn or cocoa, be of uniform, gradable quality so the buyer and seller both know what is being exchanged. But live cattle were difficult to grade—it took a cattle-buyer's eye to understand the fluid characteristics that would translate into a tasty, tender burger or sizzling steak. And fourth, "storability" is another key component of commodities exchange. Grain can be stored in a grain elevator until leaner times and then sold at a profit. "You can't store a herd of live animals for a month," detractors protested. At first, many of the traders, particularly the old-school egg traders, thought the idea of live cattle futures was absolutely ridiculous, and meats became the domain of the younger, hungrier men.[25]

The fact also remained that during the 1950s and onward, Americans were eating more beef. The meat packers and processors needed a way to hedge their risk; the exchange saw a way to create a profitable product. Therefore, on November 30, 1964, just before the opening bell, a Chicago Merc employee led a Black Angus steer onto the trading floor, compliments of Colonel Herman E. Lacy of Shamrock Farms in McHenry, Illinois. The steer was flanked by Glenn Andersen and Merc president E. B. Harris, both decked out in Texas-style garb, complete with bolo ties and ten-gallon hats.[26] The live cattle–futures contract was launched. At first, business was slow, but it soon picked up, to the point that the rival CBOT took notice. Many cattlemen traded corn futures because they used corn as feed—adding cattle futures would create a one-stop shop, CBOT officials reasoned. In his 2009 memoir, former Merc chairman Leo Melamed recalls the hyper-competition that resulted between the two Chicago exchanges:

> In an attempt not to be left out of the meat market, the CBOT launched a steer carcass beef contract six months later. To retaliate, the CME quickly launched a dressed beef contract. Both contracts failed. Then, on April 15, 1966, Warren Lebeck, president of the CBOT, announced plans to compete with the CME by also launching a live cattle contract. It created quite a stir in Chicago, causing some real bad blood between the two exchanges. Merc president Everette B. Harris accused the CBOT of violating an "unwritten law of commodity futures trading which limits the trading of one commodity to a single exchange in the same city." As far as I could tell, old E.B. Harris invented that rule on the spot.[27]

Trading in live cattle began at the CBOT on October 4, 1966. The "competitive fray" lasted for five years.

Pork belly trade came first to the Chicago marts in 1961 and has its own set of stories. But it is worth noting that pork bellies traded sluggishly at first, until live cattle futures helped goose the market. With traders able to speculate on the relative price changes of bellies and beef, the belly market began to thrive. By 1967, bellies became the exchange's first million-contract commodity. For the first time, meatpacking firms, feeders, and ranchers joined the exchange as clearing members. The biggest pits on the exchange floor belonged to cattle and pork bellies. Suddenly, meat was the wave of the future. The striking success earned pork bellies a reputation as "the contract that built the Chicago Mercantile Exchange." But the belly contract could not have been a winner without the live cattle contract, which then-president E. B. Harris called "my monument."

Why were cattle futures such an instant success when pork bellies had such a slow start? According to Mark Powers, the Merc's first economist, an accessible image had a lot to do with it: "Public speculators knew what a steer looked like and knew that steers became steaks," he explained. "Trading in live beef futures conjured up romantic images of old west cattle drives and cowboys. People who bought futures felt just like the cattle barons."[28]

Fortuitous timing also helped the success of the cattle contracts, launched just as the nation's cattle feeders were reeling from nearly two years of depressed markets. Further, Americans were beginning to eat more beef, a trend that would carry through the 1970s and beyond.

After the standard live cattle contract proved its staying power, other cattle-driven trading vehicles soon followed. In the late 1960s, the "boneless beef" contract was formed, followed by feeder cattle contracts debuted in 1971. The "feeder cattle" term refers to young "yearling" cattle, which are mature enough to be separated and fattened in a feedlot before being slaughtered. The product was the brainchild of E. B. Harris, who argued that "cattle in a feedlot of uniform quality were just as much in storage as graded cotton in a mill or wheat in an elevator," and therefore could be considered an "inventory risk that had to be protected." Harris secured quick approval for live cattle futures from his buddies at the Commodity Exchange Authority, and they were an immediate success.[29]

Those feeder cattle contracts continue to have relevancy today. Jumping ahead to the modern day for a moment, consider the ties between one of the largest consumers (and traders) of beef—McDonald's Corporation—and

FEEDER CATTLE VERSUS FAT CATTLE

Betty Fussell explains well how feeder cattle versus live cattle contracts interact in the trading world:

> The only "real" price in the cattle market is the fed-cattle price: the price the cow sells for at the moment of slaughter. . . . Fifty-some years ago, when prices were less volatile than now, most cattle feeders owned the cattle they fed because there was no futures market. A rancher's best road to profit was to buy heifers at the bottom of the cycle when they were cheap and sell them as grown cows at the top of the cycle. Feeders were priced against each day's fat-cattle price, so that profit and loss could be calculated before the animal was fed. The price difference in the feedlot between incoming "feeder" cattle and outgoing "fat" cattle is still called the "swap." When grain is cheap, the supply of feeder cattle will expand and necessarily lower the price of fat cattle.*

*Betty Fussell, *Raising Steaks: The Life and Times of American Beef* (Orlando, Fla.: Harcourt, 2008), 144–145.

feeder cattle contracts. The world's largest restaurant chain announced in 2011 plans to open one outlet each day in China, Asia's largest economy.[30] Unsurprisingly, feeder cattle prices surged on the anticipated increase in demand for beef. If that trajectory continues unchecked, it can result in higher wholesale and retail prices for beef, and ultimately, inflated prices for hamburgers at McDonald's and elsewhere. (A side note: although it's tempting to try to tie cattle futures to the hamburger industry alone, it is worth noting that the packing industry's most valuable product—more so than even beef—is cattle hides. American exports of cowhides bring more than $1 billion in foreign trade, and U.S. finished-leather production is worth about $4 billion.)[31]

In 1971, the same year feeder cattle contracts debuted, another seminal event took place: the stockyards in Chicago closed, and a bulldozer razed the pens that once held the hogs and the cattle. With that, one of the last physical ties to the old frontier days disappeared. Today, all that remains is the arched limestone gate through which millions of cattle once passed on their way to Packer Town.

What Trades Now

- *Feeder Cattle*: Trades on the CME. Contract size is 50,000 pounds (23 metric tons). When calves are about six to ten months old and are ready to be placed in feedlots, they are referred to as "feeder cattle." Once a feeder calf enters a feedlot, there is intense focus on feeding the calf for slaughter—the animal's average number of days on feed is 150.[32]
- *Live Cattle*: Trades on the CME. Contract size is 40,000 pounds (18 metric tons). After an animal is finished with the feeding process, it can be traded as live cattle (some call them "fat cattle" or "fed cattle") rather than feeder cattle. Live-weight pricing is based on estimated carcass weights and quality (generally "prime," "choice," "select," and "standard") and yield grades (1 through 5, with the higher numbers representing a lower proportion of salable retail cuts from the carcass). The CME futures contract specifies "55% Choice, 45% Select, Yield Grade 3 live steers."[33]

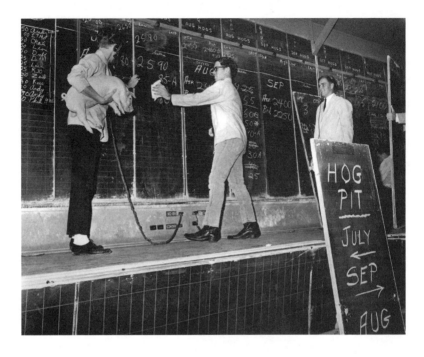

Opening day of the live hog contract at the Chicago Mercantile Exchange (February 28, 1966). (Image used with the permission of CME Group Inc. © 2011. All rights reserved.)

CHAPTER EIGHT

This Little Piggy Made a Market

The Rise and Fall of Pork Bellies

Have you ever seen this cartoon? It's a household scene at dinner,
and the wife says, "Pork bellies are not proper dinner conversation."
LEO MELAMED, FORMER CHAIRMAN OF THE CHICAGO MERCANTILE EXCHANGE

Bacon: we know it, love it, lust after it, obsess over it (and, in a recent
TV commercial, marry it). However, we forget that it is essentially pork
belly—cured, smoked, and fried into a delectably crisp, salty breakfast side,
guaranteed to wake an entire household with its seductive, savory aroma.
But traders know. And for fifty years, they counted on our collective bacon
obsession, to profitable effect.

As a financial instrument, pork bellies were iconic. For many, the image
of greedy traders as pigs at the trough was equally iconic. Until pork belly
became a headliner on restaurant menus recently, few knew exactly what
a pork belly was. Pork bellies created a viable market at a precarious time
for the Chicago Mercantile Exchange, and they lasted for a half-century,
until the market closed in July 2011.

Defining the Pork Belly

So what exactly is a pork belly? It is the meat carved from the underside of
the abdomen and the chest of the pig, which consists of alternating layers
of fat and lean muscle. Pork belly is widely used in making sausage, paté,

and terrines. It is increasingly cooked as a luscious, fatty dish in its own right. Cured and cut into strips, pork belly becomes bacon.

To traders, a hog technically has two "bellies," which are cut off in slabs and then frozen in storage until sliced for bacon. And from each mature hog ready for slaughter, a measly 12 to 15 percent of that is belly—which explains why it is considered relatively precious. A little useless trivia: one hog yields approximately 250 bacon, lettuce, and tomato sandwiches, depending on the size of the animal (and the heft of your BLT). Compared with harder "back fat" (the cut of the pig that yields Canadian bacon), belly fat is the softest and most succulent found on the animal—another reason it has been valued so highly throughout history.

Americans aren't the only ones who have had a love affair with pork. Although it is hard to know for certain, historians say the Chinese were likely the first to taste roast pork (and pork belly continues to be featured on Chinese menus). In ancient Greece, pork was a mainstay of banquet feasts. Romans of all classes were fond of pork, and Roman historian Pliny the Elder noted that a talented cook could derive more than fifty different flavors from pork.

When European settlers came to the New World, they found that pork was the favorite and most widely consumed meat, and this continued to be the case well into the twentieth century. Farmers liked pigs: the animals required little management, fattened swiftly, and were easier to handle than cattle because they were smaller and therefore easier to kill and cure. The flesh preserved well using materials that were easy to obtain—salt, sugar, and smoke—which meant it could be stored for later consumption in an era without home refrigeration.

Trading

Long before Wall Street became a commercial center, it owed its name to hogs. Free-roaming hogs were famous for rampaging through the valuable grain fields of colonial New York City. The Manhattan Island residents chose to block the troublesome hogs with a long wall on the northern edge of what is now lower Manhattan (though according to other accounts, that wall was built to keep out Native American inhabitants). A street came to border this wall: Wall Street, now known as the financial center of the United States.

As with most agricultural products, trading of hogs and pork parts began as a relatively informal affair and gradually became more organized, with prices listed in the papers. Early newspaper accounts of "commercial and money affairs" typically included a paragraph under the bloodless heading "provisions"—which included listings of prices for hogs and cattle. For pork, in addition to listings for lard and "pickled meats," prices would reflect the availability of pork shoulders and "sides"—the same underportion of the pig that would be cured for bacon and which we now refer to as pork belly.

The Rise and Fall of Porkopolis

Because the Midwest was home to so many farms, much of the trading naturally took place there, and then animals and their parts would be shipped to the more populous eastern towns. Most of America's pork is still produced by the midwestern states of Iowa, Minnesota, Illinois, and Indiana, which together generate half of the total U.S. hog revenues.[1]

In addition to cultivating and slaughtering livestock, packing and preserving the flesh was the biggest challenge meat packers faced. "Decay was the great enemy of the meat-packer," wrote William Cronon, "wasting an investment in fatted hogs and steers more quickly than the animals lost weight on a long drive. . . . Preventing such waste was the chief task of the packer."[2] The meatpacking industry of the Great West began not with cattle but with hogs. There were several good reasons for this. Up until the 1870s (the advent of refrigeration), the best available means for halting natural decay—salt and smoke—were much more effective with pork than with beef. Further, most Americans preferred their steaks fresh. Pork, on the other hand, had been salted and smoked since colonial times, and many of its most eagerly sought forms were packed rather than fresh: bacon, ham, sausage, lard, and various sorts of pickled pork. Cattle, with their long legs and easygoing natures, were relatively easy to drive to market; hogs, meanwhile, despite their smaller size, were more difficult to handle in terms of temperament and they lost weight quickly while on the road. Thus, there were strong economic incentives to slaughter and pack pigs where the farmers raised them.

Most pork-packing operations were small and enjoyed few economies of scale. But packing in Cincinnati was the exception. The city is located at the confluence of several major rivers, which drew to it produce from the wide farming region of Ohio, Indiana, and Kentucky. By the 1830s, Cincinnati was the largest pork-packing city in North America and proudly called itself Porkopolis.

Just as the grain elevator would revolutionize the corn and grain industries, novel manufacturing techniques—pioneered in Cincinnati—would transform the meatpacking industry. The earliest step toward mechanization was a large horizontal wheel from which pig carcasses hung. As it rotated, workers at the eight points of its compass cleaned and gutted the animals in eight separate steps before sending them off to a storage room for cooling. Once cold, they were taken to tables where master butchers systematically cut them into pieces to be packed and marketed. The whole system came to be called "the disassembly line."[3]

Perhaps the most powerful description of the disassembly line came from journalist and landscape architect Frederick Law Olmsted, who visited Cincinnati in the winter of 1853/1854:

> We entered an immense low-ceilinged room and followed a vista of dead swine, upon their backs, their paws stretching mutely toward heaven. Walking down to the vanishing point, we found there a sort of human chopping-machine where the hogs were converted into commercial pork. A plank table, two men to lift and turn, two to wield the cleavers, were its component parts. No iron cog-wheels could work with more regular motion. Plump falls the hog upon the table, chop, chop; chop, chop; chop, chop, fall the cleavers. All is over. But, before you can say so, plump, chop, chop; chop, chop, sounds again. . . . Amazed beyond all expectation at the celerity, we took out our watches and counted thirty-five seconds, from the moment when one hog touched the table until the next occupied its place.[4]

"The very air smells of pork," another writer from New York observed. "The entire business of preparing pork for market is reduced to a system which astonishes the uninitiated. A live, comfortable, well-to-do hog is, in the short space of *three* minutes, as stiff as a poker, and hanging [like a] pendent from a spike, *sans* bristles, *sans* liver; changed from a low-bred, filthy creature, to good merchantable pork—a thing for shrewd, bustling merchants to talk about on 'Change.'"[5]

However, Porkopolis and its disassembly line would soon prove to have flaws. Among them was the fact that the disassembly line relied primarily on human labor rather than the new mechanical technologies, and it was dependent on seasonality. Cincinnati did most of its hog-packing work in winter, when the natural cold could slow meat's decay, leaving its immense plant idle for the rest of the year.

At the start of the 1850s, Chicago packed 20,000 hogs, compared with Cincinnati's 334,000.[6] But as the railroads extended west, the landscape began to shift. Midwest communities could now ship their animals eastward via Chicago rather than southward through the river towns. The Civil War further cemented Chicago's dominance of the American pork-packing industry. One and a half million men enlisted in the Union Army during the war; while in the field, they consumed more than 500 million pounds of packed meat. At the same time, the Union blockade of the lower Mississippi closed off from western farmers their ordinary produce regions—New Orleans and the southern cotton country. With unsalable corn on their hands, they had little choice but to feed it to their pigs. Chicago benefited from increases in both supply and demand. Its pork-packing industry exploded during the war, while Cincinnati's grew by less than half. In 1862, Chicago pushed ahead of Cincinnati to become the world's largest pork-packing center, and by the early 1870s, it was processing considerably more than a million hog carcasses a year.[7]

Chicago Stockyards

For Chicago to supplant Cincinnati as Porkopolis was no easy feat, but the City of Big Shoulders was the beneficiary of several well-timed developments. First and foremost was the railroad, which brought hogs (and other livestock and produce) in and swiftly shipped them out as processed, salable commodities. Second was the Civil War, which further clinched supply and demand. Third was advancing refrigeration technologies, critical for preserving and transporting livestock commodities without spoilage. Chicago had long used winter ice, cut from the Chicago River and nearby ponds, to keep stored meat and other perishables cool. But as the railroads came into play, ice from the lakes that ringed the city in Illinois and Indiana could be used to cool perishables shipped by rail—meaning that pork packing could continue even into the summer months, and farmers could now count on finding a year-round market in Chicago for their corn-fattened

THE LORD OF LARD

Another pig product, lard, enjoyed a strong trading market in the late nineteenth century. However, the backhanded efforts of Chicago trader Peter McGeoch led to an outcry that helped hasten the arrival of the Pure Food and Drug Act a couple of decades later.

McGeoch first made his fortune in wheat, cornering the Milwaukee market in 1878. He later joined with future meat packer P. D. Armour and others in a spectacular and controversial wheat corner in 1882. But pork was what captured his attention. "Flushed with victory and money," William Ferris writes in *The Grain Traders*, "McGeoch decided later that year to engineer a little corner of his own in lard."* He became such a dominant player in the market, the newspapers referred to him as "The Lord of Lard."

By June 1, 1883, McGeoch was credited with owning 200,000 tierces of cash lard and being long 600,000 tierces of lard futures. (One tierce contained about 320 pounds and was a standard measure of capacity used for packing lard.) When it came time to take delivery, he refused, claiming it was not "pure" lard. Board rules defined pure lard as consisting of nothing but hog fat. Refiners in Chicago also produced what was known as "refined lard," which consisted of hog fat but also tallow (the harder fat of sheep and cattle, used to make candles and soap) and, it was sometimes charged,

pigs. The development of ice-cooled railway cars in the 1870s also meant that the chilled meat could be transferred east, with some shipments (although primarily cattle, not pork) even bound for other continents. And fourth was the tireless effort to use every single part of the animal, stretching pork efficiencies as far as they could possibly go, combating waste and maximizing profit. As pork- and beef-packing giant P. D. Armour was fond of saying, "We use everything in the hog except the squeal."[8]

This push for efficiency also extended to trading, once it was determined that a centralized marketplace would be the smartest course. For years, shippers moved their animals through crowded streets to reach one of the several small stockyards scattered among the various districts in southern Chicago. In the 1840s and 1850s, the hotels adjacent to the stockyards became legendary. There, drovers lodged and entertained themselves while cottonseed oil. Refined lard was considerably cheaper than pure lard. An investigation was ordered.

An uproar in the newspapers followed, stoking public distrust in lard purity, which created a panic in the financial markets, driving prices lower. Meanwhile, McGeoch still owned most of the lard, both that in store and that which would be delivered in the future. In the end, the market for lard crashed. Even with a partial bailout from Armour, McGeoch lost millions of dollars. "I am now about as poor as a man can be," McGeoch lamented shortly after the collapse, although his poverty was likely overstated, as he was part owner of the Milwaukee Railway Company. In 1895, McGeoch shot himself. "He died covered in blood, but with a large diamond in his cravat."[†]

Another outcome of the scandal: several states passed laws prohibiting adulteration of lard. Furthermore, Canada, Mexico, and some European countries banned American lard outright. McGeoch's attempted corner arrived at a time of reformist agitation against adulterated foods, but it was not until 1907 that a Pure Food and Drug Act became effective, prohibiting adulteration or misbranding of food and drugs.

[*]William G. Ferris, *The Grain Traders: The Story of the Chicago Board of Trade* (East Lansing: Michigan State University Press, 1988), 65.
[†]Ibid., 73.

completing their transactions; money gained from hog sales often flowed directly to the copious restaurants, saloons, and brothels located conveniently nearby[9]—yet another economy created by the livestock trade.

However, the coming of the railroads changed the landscape. By the mid-1850s, most of the stockyards had rail connections that enabled shippers to send packed meat and live animals east. Like the grain elevators, individual yards had connections with only one or two railroads, and their scattered locations made it difficult for drovers to move among them, shepherding cattle or hogs along. Wrote one observer: "A drover bringing a herd of cattle or hogs into the market, was obliged to drive them through the crowded streets of the city, to yard after yard, thereby suffering the greatest inconvenience, and in many instances loss, occasioned by the difficulty of driving, and rough pavements, which lacerated and tore the hoofs of the animals, producing disease and other evils."[10] Further, the fragmented market made it difficult for buyers and sellers to compare the prices being offered in different yards, and even financial reporters for the city's newspapers had trouble gathering accurate information about price movements. The problem reached crisis proportions in the early years of the Civil War, when the Union Army's demand for provisions led Chicago to surpass Cincinnati as the largest meat packer in the world.

The solution—a single, centralized stockyard—was proposed in the fall of 1864, when Chicago's nine largest railroads, in conjunction with members of the Chicago Pork Packers Association, issued a prospectus for what they called the Union Stock Yard and Transit Company.[11] The Union Stock Yard opened for business on Christmas Day in 1865.[12] It sat upon 345 acres, was paved smoothly to facilitate the flow of the livestock, and contained oblong pens—a large number of those constructed to hold precisely one carload of livestock. Six hay barns and six corn cribs would feed the animals. And most important, nine of the principal railroads found a common center in the stockyard.[13]

The Stock Yard was intersected by a new sixty-six-foot-wide "Broadway," which led from the elegant Hough House hotel to the Exchange Building. At one end, the former stockyard hotels found centralization, in the form of the Hough House, which stood six stories high and contained 260 rooms for livestock dealers and their guests. From the south side of the hotel, "the most delightful view is afforded of the prairie, which rolls away southward in one unbroken sea of land." City views dominated from the north and east sides; directly below, viewers could see "the great bovine city, with its thousands of cattle and swine, and restless flow of traffic."[14] Next to the hotel stood the yellow limestone structure known as the Exchange Building. During the 1860s, it contained a bank that regularly handled up to $500,000 worth of transactions each day, as well as telegraph facilities that gathered meat prices and livestock news from every corner of the globe. Its most important feature, though, was the great hall, where dealers conducted their daily business in much the same way as the grain traders at the Board of Trade.[15] (Although it seems logical that this should have evolved later into a full-fledged futures exchange—perhaps a predecessor to the Chicago Mercantile Exchange—this did not come to pass.)

By most accounts, the Chicago stockyards and particularly the "disassembly line" that rose up to slaughter and process the animals was a grisly place. Upton Sinclair provided the most famous passage ever written about the scene: "One could not stand and watch very long without becoming philosophical, without beginning to deal in symbols and similes, and to hear the hog-squeal of the universe."[16] Considering this porcine geography, it is only natural that the majority of pork belly futures trade migrated to the Merc. And it was a hefty contract: each one called for the physical delivery of 40,000 pounds (about 18 metric tons) of frozen pork bellies, which were slaughtered at USDA federally inspected slaughtering plants.

Civil War

A very few historians point to the Civil War era as a precursor for pork belly trading—although this is largely forgotten in most institutional accounts of trading history. William Cronon notes that during the Civil War, "the Union army's demand for oats and pork generated a huge speculative market in those commodities, which finally helped institutionalize futures trading as a standard feature of the Chicago Board of Trade. It was no accident that the Board adopted its first formal rules governing futures contracts in 1865."[17]

According to Tamarkin's history of the Merc, former CME chairman Leo Melamed often kept company with "an elderly, cigar-chomping bachelor" named Elmer Falker, who had known Melamed since his days as a young Merrill Lynch runner in the 1950s.[18] It was Falker who would recall a decade later that pork bellies had traded at the CBOT during the Civil War; salt pork or so-called sow bellies were a soldier's main provision. Although this is not well documented, it is certainly possible that the knowledge that a precursor existed for pork bellies helped cement the Merc's decision to give them a go in the 1960s.

Pork Bellies Save the Merc's Bacon

Since the Merc was the center of the pork belly universe, I called on the experts there to tell me more about why we traded pork bellies at all. I was fortunate to arrange an interview with Leo Melamed, who told me the story of how pork bellies saved the once-foundering exchange.

In the late 1950s, the Merc was not doing well. After thriving in earlier years as the scrappy Butter and Egg Board, the exchange was facing steep competition from its patrician rival, the CBOT, which had developed a booming business in soybeans, wheat, and other key grains. Further complicating things, the Merc was reeling from a scandal related to once-lucrative onion futures. In 1959, onion trading was outlawed, and trading in eggs and butter had largely dried up. The Merc fell into a period of decline. "The place was draped in black," Melamed recalled, describing the eerie quiet at the Merc. "It was like going to a funeral every day."[19]

A new committee was formed to consider new contracts, led by Glenn H. Andersen, president of Andco, one of the largest commodity brokerage firms in Chicago. ("He knew something about meats," Melamed quipped.)[20] Under Andersen's stewardship, the CME started to change course: while the CBOT retained its dominance in the grains space, the Merc became the expert on livestock, initiating trade in pork bellies—and later cattle and hog futures. The *New York Times* reported on the development with obvious glee: "Long famous as the nation's trading center for egg futures, [the CME] plans to add bacon to its diet."[21]

However, the contract almost wasn't called "pork bellies"—the term was used by the slaughterhouses and pork processors, and white-collar financiers derided the term as unseemly and disgusting.[22] Critics suggested naming the contract "uncured bacon," and some early press reports referred to "bacon in the rough." One radio announcer went with the cutesy "pork tummies." Some traders thought the name was meant as a joke. But in the end, the term widely used in the industry, "pork bellies," stuck.

The Merc began trading institutionalized pork belly futures on September 18, 1961, joining trade on the commodities exchange in shell eggs and frozen eggs, potatoes, and turkeys. By 1964, pork belly futures ascended to become one of the most popular and volatile futures on the exchange floor. Soon, live hog futures were added to the hopping frozen pork belly and skinned ham futures. Summer was a particular boom time for pork bellies—as summer tomatoes ripened, pork experts reasoned, the demand for BLT sandwiches would skyrocket, sending pork belly prices skyrocketing too.

In 1971, trading in pork belly futures began for the first time in the East by the International Commercial Exchange in New York. The contract unit was half the size of the 36,000-pound contract traded on the CME and was marketed as an "ideal" hedging instrument "for the numerous smaller and moderate-size hog slaughterers, bacon curers and slicers."[23]

A Revolution at the Supermarket

Compared with the pork belly Wild West of the early 1960s, the tone of trading in the 1970s was considerably more sober. A meat shortage, coupled with rising concerns about cholesterol, erased bacon from many Americans' shopping lists.

In 1972, Earl "Rusty" Butz, President Richard Nixon's second secretary of agriculture, helped arrange the sale of 30 million tons of American grain to Russia, which had suffered a series of disastrous harvests. It was hoped that the sale would give a boost to U.S. crop prices and help Nixon nail down the farm vote for his reelection. The unexpected surge in demand, coinciding with a spell of bad weather in the Farm Belt, drove grain prices to historic heights. Nixon was reelected, but by the following year, price inflation worked its way up the food chain to the supermarket. Some farmers were forced to kill livestock because they couldn't afford to buy feed; some foods became scarce; and the price of beef and pork soared beyond the reach of middle-class consumers. By 1973, the inflation rate for groceries reached an all-time high, and housewives organized protests at supermarkets. At the Merc, trading was disrupted in commodity futures, especially in frozen pork bellies.[24]

Dwindling stocks of stored bellies meant that traders who had contracted to deliver bellies in July and August were hard pressed to locate sufficient quantities to meet their obligations. In normal trading, futures contracts are very rarely held to the point of making delivery on or taking delivery of the actual commodity. However, government price controls and reduced supplies meant bellies trading was anything but normal. Just as traders felt the aftershocks of consumers' outcry, spiking inflation and government price controls had raised awareness of the link between commodities prices and the product on supermarket shelves. The commodities exchange and the grocery store suddenly were seen as inextricably connected. Public interest in commodities grew as never before, spurred by general concern with the rapidly increasing cost of food and the dramatic potential for profit and loss offered in the futures market. Television crews carted their cameras onto the trading floor of major commodity exchanges to show the frantic activity. Housewives even picketed the Merc because they believed it was forcing prices up.[25]

A 1973 *Chicago Tribune* article highlights the growing intensity of the situation: "One suburban housewife told her grocer that she would not pay $1.40 for bacon because 'pork bellies were down the limit and bacon had to follow.'"[26] She was right. And because she and other housewives refused to buy at the higher prices, retail prices soon headed downward.

Bellies Get Lean and Mean

By 1977, bellies prices had plunged 25 percent from earlier highs, driven by a seasonal glut and a newer, more pervasive issue: consumer health concerns about the dangers of cholesterol. The early-1980s fitness craze that spawned the desire for such things as exercise videos by über-aerobicized Jane Fonda is a good metaphor for what happened in the pork industry at around the same time. Like Fonda, pigs (and bacon) became significantly trimmer. In fact, hog farmers deliberately began breeding leaner animals to meet demand for leaner bacon. But a leaner hog means a leaner belly, and many processors found it difficult and wasteful to cure and slice slabs weighing less than 10 pounds, preferring 14- to 16-pound slabs.

To meet the demand for leaner pork, hog raisers needed to feed their animals for longer periods. Instead of marketing 180-pound or 190-pound hogs, they would have to wait until the animals weighed 230 pounds to produce the pork bellies that the processors liked. A leaner hog also yields less lard. While some processors complained bitterly that lard supplies were diminished by as much as half, commercial bakers and health-conscious cooks rejected the unhealthy fat, seeking an alternative in soybean oil and sparking a run-up in soybean contracts. Pork bellies were relatively stable in the decades that followed, weathering typical market ups and downs. But in 1998, a glut again pushed pork prices down to their lowest levels since the Depression, and some farmers started to get out of the pork belly business. By 2004, the number of hog farms had dropped 35 percent from 1998 levels, to about 73,600 farms.[27]

The time was right for small farmers to step in with heirloom hog breeds and artisan curing techniques.

Getting Pork Bellies Back on the Plate

After pork belly entered the mainstream financial lexicon, it would take another thirty years before it was established in the culinary vocabulary. If you look at restaurant menus today, you can't swing a pig without hitting pork belly on one menu or another.

From 1961, when pork belly trading officially began, until a few years ago, pork belly rarely appeared on mainstream menus or in middle-class kitchens. Granted, in some culinary circles, pork belly never went out of fashion. Some country-inspired French restaurants still served it, quietly, and it was featured in Asian dishes and southern cooking. Celebrity chef Tom Colicchio served braised pork belly at Gramercy Tavern in New York City, but he called it "fresh bacon" to make it sound more appetizing.[28] (Sound familiar? The CME didn't want to call it "pork belly" either.) Of course, bacon—an end-product of the pork belly—never went away.

But then an amazing thing happened. The new millennium began, and pork belly staged a revival on American tables. The revival was driven by a perfect storm of events. A post–September 11 restaurant downturn led some to search for cheaper cuts of meat. And a rising British-led regard for offal and eating "the whole beast" meant that pork belly and other unusual cuts were haute cuisine.[29] Furthermore, well-known French chefs, like Daniel Boulud, began prominently featuring pork belly on their menus. Also, the high-protein Atkins diet sent weight-conscious Americans on a meat-eating binge. Then, in 2003, an outbreak of mad-cow disease and high beef prices gave cheaper pork a boost, and the fusion of Asian and Mediterranean cuisines drove more pork belly dishes into the mainstream.

Journalists began writing odes to pork belly. Soon, Charlie Trotter's namesake restaurant in Chicago began serving roasted pork belly; Manhattan's Savoy offered braised pork belly, served up with loin of pork and spaetzle; and in the hands of experimental, risk-taking Wylie Dufresne, pork belly was paired with black soybeans and turnips at WD-50 in Manhattan.[30] A few restaurants still preferred to serve "braised fresh bacon"— that euphemism for "pork belly." Everywhere, pork belly was roasted, braised, shredded: clearly, this little piggy was having a very big moment in the culinary spotlight. And in a backlash to the 1970s lobby for leaner pork, chefs now roared for fattier, more flavorful hogs. How much leaner had pigs become? According to the USDA, in 1950, a pig yielded about 33.2 pounds of fat; by 1990, this figure had fallen to just 10.1 pounds.[31]

Some restaurants began to contract with small, specialized livestock farms for rare breeds of pigs and other animals. For example, Flying Pigs Farm, Niman Ranch, and others rose to cult prominence by providing to restaurant owners corpulent heritage pigs, such as Large Blacks, Gloucestershire Old Spots, and Tamworths. Chef Dan Barber raised his own Berkshire breed on the grounds of Blue Hill at Stone Barns, his farm-restaurant in Pocantico Hills, New York.[32] Home cooks sought out more pork. Supermarkets ratcheted up prices for steak (prompted in part by demand from Atkins dieters and also by dwindling supplies brought on by the fear of mad-cow disease). By comparison, the cost of pork was significantly lower versus beef.

The Demise of Pork Bellies

Despite the resurgence of pork on the plate, as 2011 dawned, experts began to predict that the contract was no longer needed—a mere fifty years after its introduction. "The pork belly is in danger of going belly-up," the *Wall Street Journal* snarked, noting that trading volume had fallen precipitously.[33]

Just as technological advances drove egg futures out of circulation, necessitating the invention of pork belly futures, now technology was driving out pork bellies too, explains Ron Plain, professor of agricultural economics at the University of Missouri and an expert in livestock trading. According to Plain, it is now possible to keep fresh, not frozen, bellies on hand, "which means we don't have huge amounts in bellies in cold storage as we used to."[34] In turn, that alleviates concern about how the condition of bellies might change between the time they are put in and taken out of storage—the very condition that would need hedging against.

Without the need to offset that risk, Plain says, "We've got a more stable pork belly situation." Unfortunately, stability doesn't attract traders and speculators, who thrive on buying and selling as volatile prices ping-pong. "Less interest from speculators and less interest from hedgers who own pork bellies in cold storage has led to few trades, and some days, no trades in pork belly contracts."[35]

Thinking back to the housewives who picketed the Merc when bacon prices ballooned at supermarkets—as pork belly futures fade into the sunset, will this affect prices at grocery stores? According to Jim Robb, director of the Livestock Marketing Information Center in Denver, the answer is no. However, it may be more difficult for bacon processors to establish a baseline price for pork products—the concept that economists term "price discovery." Explains Robb, "It helps us discover the supply and demand, what the price could be in the marketplace."[36]

So in other words, the demise of pork belly futures has led to the end of a venerable piece of financial and cultural history. It has also meant that pork belly traders needed to find a new game to play in the agricultural pits at the Chicago exchanges. The end of pork bellies might translate into slightly higher prices at the butcher because the big meat-processing companies are losing a financial leveraging tool. The end of these futures, on the other hand, might make artisanal bacon a little more attractive.

The average bacon lover barely noticed a blip on the supermarket checkout screen as pork bellies went belly-up on July 15, 2011. Like the obsolete onion and egg futures before them, pork belly contracts faded away into history, leaving behind barely a squeal of protest.

What Trades Now

- *Lean Hogs*: Trades on the CME. Contract size is 40,000 pounds (18 metric tons) of lean hog carcasses.[37]

Apple traders in action at the Chicago Mercantile Exchange (1949). (Image used with the permission of CME Group Inc. © 2011. All rights reserved.)

CHAPTER NINE

When Money Grows on Trees

Produce Futures

Now, what are commodities? Commodities are agricultural products . . .
like coffee that you had for breakfast . . . wheat, which is used to make bread
. . . pork bellies, which is used to make bacon, which you might find in
a bacon and lettuce and tomato sandwich. . . . And then there are other
commodities, like frozen orange juice . . . and GOLD. Though, of course,
gold doesn't grow on trees like oranges.
MORTIMER DUKE, IN *TRADING PLACES*

Surely, you've heard this stern warning before: "Money doesn't grow on
trees." But in the case of produce futures, money most certainly does grow
on trees . . . and on vines and below ground too. By the late nineteenth
century, both New York and Chicago had produce exchanges. San Francisco and Los Angeles also formed produce exchanges; so did Boston, in
the form of the Boston Fruit and Produce Exchange. Although the "produce exchange" moniker hasn't been used since the 1970s, when the New
York Produce Exchange was folded into the International Commercial
Exchange, produce contracts ranging from potatoes to onions to orange
juice have played a tremendous part in shaping futures exchanges. Some,
like onions, have a stinky and scandalous past, while others, like citrus
futures, have even played a starring role in popular culture.

The New York Produce Exchange

The New York Produce Exchange is the oldest of all the agglomerated
exchanges that make up modern trading organizations and has several

noteworthy antecedents. Its earliest participants were the Dutch burghers of New Amsterdam who gathered to trade essential commodities, such as grain and provisions. By 1658, the small group of farmers trading these products had moved from Bowling Green to what is now Broad Street, creating the Broadway Shambles Market. The first building known as an exchange was erected in 1691 at the foot of Broad Street. It consolidated other, smaller markets in the area, creating a centralized marketplace, and gradually became known as the Exchange. In 1752, a grander structure was built at Broad and Water Streets and became known as the Royal Exchange, sometimes referred to as the Merchants Exchange. By 1827, more room was needed, so a new building for the Merchants Exchange (as it was now exclusively called) was erected on Wall Street (and rebuilt after a fire in 1835). Soon after, the trading was relocated to a warehouse, and the Corn Exchange was born in 1853. However, the Corn Exchange was not terribly successful. The warehouse was deemed unsuitable for trading, and a few merchants monopolized activity. In 1860, a corporation known as the New York Produce Exchange Company was formed for the purposes of erecting a suitable building for the burgeoning exchange; the building was completed in 1861. A second entity not in the group formed the New York Commercial Association (NYCA) and established its own rules and trading floor at 39 Whitehall Street.[1]

Eventually, the NYCA became the New York Produce Exchange, a name it would retain for nearly a century. Expanding membership soon forced it to seek new quarters. Ten architects vied for the contract, and a red-brick building of modified Italian Renaissance design conceived by George B. Post was selected. It was built with rope-geared hydraulic lifts and a magnificent sixty-foot-high skylight. Trading rings were furnished with ornate wooden desks and blackboard slates for chalking up contract prices. In its later years, the building became known as the "Grand Old Lady of Bowling Green."[2]

What traded at the Produce Exchange? Not just produce. The *New York Times* listed the following trades on opening day:

78 bbls [barrels] Ashes (Pots and Pearls)
11,470 bbls Flour
11,482 bushels Corn
1,088 bushels barley

750 bushels Oat
1,624 pkgs Provisions (Pork, Beef, Butter, Cheese, "Country Mess")
1,010 bbls Whisky—at 19c a gallon

Other traded contracts included grain, hay, hops, and rice.

By 1901, the list had expanded. In addition to grain, "other things that [were] handled in specified quantities for speculation [were] butter, cheese, hops, resin, tar, turpentine, cornmeal, oatmeal, rye flour, flour, buckwheat, corn, oats, barley, beef, pork, seeds, sweet cured meats, liquors and high wines, beans, flaxseed, malt, tongues, and hams."[3]

Later, around 1910, the markets for evaporated and canned fruits were particularly active in New York, Philadelphia, and Chicago. A business-page headline from the April 12, 1911, *Chicago Daily Tribune* reads "Prune Market Goes Higher: Weather Hurts French Crop." Trade in canned fruit and other products, such as canned salmon, eventually were discontinued in the 1930s after the markets were deemed "too stable" to be profitable.[4]

By the 1920s, located at 2 Broadway, off Battery Place, the Produce Exchange had become a world market for corn, wheat, barley, and oats. In his memoir *Run-Through*, John Houseman, an aspiring young trader, said the floor "looked, sounded, and smelled like something between a railroad terminal, a midway and a monkey house."[5] The scene was surely chaotic, a mash-up of various European and American accents, as merchants, brokers, exporters, and shipping agents arranged grain shipments on the spot; there was lots of pushing and shoving and messengers dispatched on errands—as everyone kept an eye on the blackboards, where clerks recorded the latest commodity prices arriving by Morse code.

The Scene in Chicago

Meanwhile, in downtown Chicago and along its riverfront, merchants gathered to buy farm product to meet the provisioning needs of the growing city. The most significant of these local markets, the Chicago Produce Exchange, opened in 1874 on the northeast corner of Clark and Lake Streets. As many as three hundred grocery dealers gathered there to buy and sell vegetables as well as butter, eggs, and other assorted dairy products.

GRAPES OF MATH: WINE FUTURES

As long as we're talking produce futures, let's consider grapes, and one of their choicest derivatives: wine. Although they don't trade on U.S. exchanges and the dynamics are a bit different from those on the commodities market, investors around the world trade wine futures.

Compared with the back-and-forth of a typical exchange, Bordeaux futures tend to trade just once, when the original buyer purchases the contract, and the prices historically don't fluctuate much. There is no central wine futures exchange in downtown Bordeaux—transactions are conducted through wine merchants in the United States and Europe. But the market has its own unique sense of drama: when the futures market opens each spring, France buzzes with excitement and activity, descending on the wine chateaux for so-called barrel tastings, in which chateau owners pull unfinished wine from the barrels to provide the first taste of what that year's effort has produced. The reports and scores that ensue can drive consumer interest and prices when the futures contracts ultimately go on sale several weeks later. (Some skeptics might even liken the frenzy to the traders and Maine potato farmers who once traveled to New York each May to watch traders duke it out in the potato pits.)

Another crucial difference between wine futures and, say, corn futures is the timing of payments. With wine, you pay for your purchase up front, eighteen to twenty-four months before the wine will be delivered. Once the wine is delivered, it can either be sold or cellared; unlike commodities marts, there is no central marketplace for buying and selling before the wine arrives.*

Some historians point to Napoleon III, who in 1855 effectively started the Fine Wine Index when he classified the wines in Bordeaux from 1 to 5, basing his decision on the quality and prices realized on each of the chateaux wines over the previous one hundred years or so. Bordeaux wines continue to rank among the most "investable," making up 90 percent of investment-grade wines worldwide,† although a handful of cult-classic California wines also make the grade for shorter-term investors.

Modern-day investors wishing to track the fine-wine market look to the London International Vintners Exchange, or Liv-ex. This Internet- and phone-based exchange was launched in 1999 and has been credited with bringing some transparency into the infamously opaque fine-wine market. Its 240 member merchants and funds can buy and sell wines (some *en primeur*—wines still in the barrel—comparable to wine futures). Each month, Liv-ex aggregates wine prices into the Liv-ex Fine Wine 100 Index, widely regarded as the wine industry's leading benchmark.[‡]

In 2009, Liv-ex estimated that wine investment activity represented $3 billion internationally; that's a drop in the spit bucket compared with other markets (the world equity market is estimated at about ten times that size, the world bond market about twenty times larger). But the fledgling market has taken off in the past five to ten years, encouraged by favorable tax regulations in some countries in Asia and Europe and savvy investors looking to diversify portfolios.

David Sokolin, a rare-wine merchant based in Bridgehampton, New York, sums up the current climate as "dynamic demand for static supply."[§] In other words, since wines are produced in limited quantities and are consumed over time, the supply becomes progressively scarcer, and as the wine matures, it often becomes more valuable and desirable. Meanwhile, the pool of consumers who would like to buy those specific valuable wines is growing in leaps and bounds.[**]

Experts point to the burgeoning Chinese market in particular, where wine is used to show hospitality to friends, as well as to signal prosperity. "The Chinese are the biggest buyers of wine in the world," asserts David Boren, investment manager of Fine Wine Investment and Wealth Fund. "And they drink it—they are not storing it for 20 years." Further, Boren estimates that China consumes wine at 8.5 liters per capita, compared with 6 liters per capita in the Western world.[††]

While investing in wine isn't for everyone, many consider it to be a "passion investment," in the words of Stacey-Lea Golding, investments director and cofounder of Premier Cru in London.[‡‡] That puts wine in the same category as luxury investments such as fine art and real estate. At least, if the fine-wine bubble eventually pops, it offers something no other collectible can claim: it can be consumed. Just try drinking a Picasso.

---

[*]David Sokolin, *Investing in Liquid Assets: Uncorking Profits in Today's Global Wine Market* (New York: Simon and Schuster, 2008), 97–98.

[†]Ibid., 133.

[‡]Vidya Ram, "Wine Futures," *Forbes Europe*, July 13, 2009.

[§]Sokolin, *Investing in Liquid Assets*, 133.

[**]David Sokolin, interview with author, August 27, 2009.

[††]David Boren, interview with author, August 21, 2009.

[‡‡]Stacey-Lea Golding, interview with author, August 21, 2009.

The Chicago Board of Trade (and the New York Produce Exchange) already traded forward, or "to arrive," contracts, for future delivery, but Chicago's Produce Exchange merchants traded only "spot," or immediate delivery, contracts and used the exchange as a handy place to meet colleagues and gather market information. In its earliest form, the exchange was more a club for produce traders than a place of business.

Interest in a formal marketplace waned, and the Chicago Produce Exchange became inactive in 1876, a mere two years after it opened. Competition from a couple of Chicago taverns, which were popular gathering places for the produce traders, diverted business from the exchange. The informal merchandising style of the time further weakened the exchange. The produce business was merely a kitchen-garden offshoot of the mighty midwestern grain machine. Produce by nature is perishable and, with the exception of eggs, was not storable or suitable for future delivery. The merchants who dealt in produce were not the robber barons of the grain exchanges. They were more likely to be newly arrived immigrants, struggling to build a family business.

Although the Chicago Produce Exchange was revived in 1884, it was merely "an agglomerate of produce dealers, egg traders, and oleomargarine dealers." By 1895, the egg-and-butter dealers split off to form their own exchange. In 1898, the Butter and Egg Board became a permanent entity, separate from the Chicago Produce Exchange.[6] Later on, this exchange would become the Chicago Mercantile Exchange.

Produce Contracts

It is fascinating to see which products were selected for trading, which thrived—if only for a while—and which withered on the vine. Here is a closer look at some of the various produce contracts—apples, onions, potatoes, tomatoes, and orange juice—that traded mid-century and beyond.

Apples

Apples started trading as early as 1949 on the Chicago Merc[7] and in 1969 on the New York Mercantile Exchange (NYMEX).[8] The contract called for domestically grown delicious, red delicious, or golden delicious apples.

It is hard to pinpoint when trading ended because the prices were rarely printed in newspapers. Apples don't ever appear to have been an active market, and trading likely thinned further until it ceased altogether.

However, in 2011 and 2012, the Minneapolis Grain Exchange was in the process of launching an apple juice–concentrate contract, with each unit representing 1,800 gallons.[9] Why? To create a hedge for the $3.2 billion industry—apparently, although apple juice is certainly made in the United States, the vast majority is produced in China, South America, and Europe. It is therefore a global product worthy of financial risk protection.

Onions

Onions played a notorious part in commodities market history: the great onion scandal of 1953 led to the outlawing of the onion trade and ushered in new, stricter trading regulations. In retrospect, it is ironic how many butter-and-egg men came to make their fortunes in Chicago, which had derived its name from *checagou*, an Algonquian word that means "wild onion"[10]—a fitting omen of things to come at the Chicago Mercantile Exchange.

At the Merc, onion futures were introduced "out of desperation" in 1942.[11] The onset of World War II revived the economy but brought price controls to the commodities markets, and it very nearly wiped out Chicago's futures exchanges. In 1943, trading volume had skidded to just 3,223 contracts, and half of that was in onion futures.[12] Because onions did not fall under price controls or within the regulatory realm of the Commodity Exchange Act, they offered a refreshingly free market to traders. But even though onion trading brought new business to the exchange, the Merc probably would have folded if not for the strong connection most members still had to the cash markets for butter, eggs, and other produce. While the war nearly snuffed out futures trading, supplying the war effort with foodstuffs kept many Merc member firms in business.[13]

"The onion market was a great success" in the 1950s, recalled former Merc Chairman Leo Melamed. "It was a perishable crop, it depended on the weather, and so it would move up and down—that was good for the markets." When E. B. Harris moved to the Merc as its president in 1953, eggs and onions were the exchange's primary markets. Of the CME's record 500,000 contracts traded in 1955, about 100,000 were onion futures, making the malodorous bulb the exchange's fastest-growing product.[14]

And that's when the Merc lost the onion contract. It was a turnkey event that sent the exchange into a tailspin, galvanizing a set of Merc members into seeking fresh leadership and eventually leading to the introduction of pork belly futures as well as a prosperous new era for the exchange. But in 1955, that was still decades away. Dominated by a few dealers and growers, and with virtually inelastic demand, onions were a market waiting for trouble. Like the egg futures before them, onion futures had been the arena for multiple cornering events and price manipulations over the years. And the Merc's onion crowd apparently saw no reason to curb their activities just because, in 1955, the Commodity Exchange Authority (CEA) claimed oversight of the onion market for the first time.[15]

Once it gained jurisdiction, the CEA promptly investigated a $1.5 million price-rigging scheme that would be one of the most spectacular market-fixing incidents in the history of the Chicago exchanges. The corner—as it turned out, the last one for onions—involved Sam S. Siegel, a Merc onion trader who owned a suburban Chicago produce company; Vincent Kosuga, a New York–based onion dealer; and a handful of unfortunate Michigan onion growers. Through aggressive selling on the Merc, the Siegel group pushed down the price of a 50-pound bag of onions from $2.55 to 10 cents between August 1955 and March 1956. At that level, traders liked to say, the onions were worth less than the string bags in which they were shipped.[16] (Everyone seems to have a story about this time in history—financial analyst Alan Bush joked, "An old-timer told me maybe twenty years ago that during the height of the onion scandal, they would dump the onions and sell the bags!")[17]

An abrupt price decline was hardly the result of free-market forces. A CEA investigation found that the collapse resulted from a traders' shoot-out in the onion market. In the fall of 1955, Kosuga had bought large quantities of November onion futures, causing the "shorts" in those contracts to ship 28 million pounds of onions into Chicago to deliver against Kosuga's long position. Meanwhile, Siegel and his produce company were also acquiring onions. By early December, Kosuga and Siegel had teamed together and had one thousand carloads of onions stored in Chicago—a total of 30 million pounds, worth about $1.5 million.[18]

In a year of onion scarcity, the accumulation of such large stocks in the hands of one or two traders might have constituted a corner that would have driven onion prices higher. But Siegel and Kosuga were done with their long position and wanted to start selling. They advised thirteen big Michigan onion growers that the onions would be dumped on the market if the growers did not step in and buy out the dealers' stocks. Fearing they would be clobbered by a price slump, the growers reluctantly took title to 265 carloads of onions, worth about $168,000—a sizable amount, but far less than the $500,000 Siegel and Kosuga had hoped to unload.[19]

As part of the deal, Kosuga and Siegel had promised the growers they would keep buying enough onions on the cash market to support futures prices on the Merc. But that wasn't the real plan. Instead, Siegel and Kosuga began shorting onion futures almost immediately after the growers bought the onions. By February 6, the two men had sold 1,148 carloads of onion futures at a price of $1.02 per bag. The short position had one problem: the onions Kosuga and Siegel held in Chicago warehouses were starting to spoil. To make them suitable for delivery in Chicago, the two dealers shipped the onions out of the city to have them cleaned and reconditioned. Seeing the onions return to Chicago, futures traders got the mistaken impression that these carloads represented significant new deliveries. The resultant selling depressed prices even further and added to the Siegel group's profits. As the March contract neared expiration, onions had skidded to 10 cents a bag.[20] Observed E. B. Harris, "Onion prices dropped to the point where the 50-pound bags that held the onions were worth more than the onions themselves."[21]

The enraged and double-crossed onion growers appealed to Congress, which opened hearings on a bill to outlaw onion futures trading even before the CEA started its investigation. Despite a strenuous outcry from the Merc and a public relations effort aimed at showcasing the benefits of onion futures, Congress, in 1958, amended the Commodity Exchange Act to abolish the onion market. One important claim behind this action was testimony that onion trading "differed in character" from the hedging of commodities such as grain, corn, or cotton. Rather than managing volatility, the CEA concluded, the speculative nature of onion trading caused "severe and unwarranted fluctuations and price," sufficient to restrict "the orderly flow of onions in interstate commerce."[22] After such a big stink, trading onion futures became a misdemeanor under federal law.[23]

Potatoes

By the standards of even the rowdy commodities market, the 1976 great potato bust was bizarre. It resulted in the one time–delivery failure of 50 million pounds of potatoes, worth $4.2 million, sending almost one thousand potato futures contracts into default.[24] This event, in turn, touched off scores of lawsuits and an investigation by government regulators. Traders who lived through the scandal are quick to note that it spelled the end of agricultural commodities trading for the New York Mercantile Exchange. Ultimately, the bust resulted in a complete about-face for the NYMEX, as it switched out of ag contracts to focus on trading in metals and energy futures, eventually becoming a leader in those markets.

Long after the butter-and-egg trading days were gone, the NYMEX became known as a potato-trading powerhouse. But through the 1970s, when Maine potatoes had come to represent 80 percent of the exchange's business,[25] there was a burgeoning mash-up in the potato market. The roughly six dozen traders working from a red-brick mansion located at 6 Harrison Street in Manhattan began receiving word of a mysterious potato shortage. Maine's annual potato crop was falling as Idaho began emerging as the new potato capital. Stories began to circulate of train cars arriving from Maine filled with bags of potato-shaped rocks instead of real potatoes and some freight cars not showing up at all. With Maine and Idaho "crashing antlers" over which state would claim potato primacy, prices went haywire, to the extreme satisfaction of the New York pit traders. Potato prices skyrocketed ever higher, but it made no difference to the traders, who reaped their profits from the gaps between buying and selling prices.[26]

Especially in the days before frozen foods, the big month for trading potatoes was May. As a longtime trader explains in Leah McGrath Goodman's account of the NYMEX:

> Potatoes were grown in the summer, harvested in the autumn, and then stored until supply ran out around May each year. That's when the supplies were the most uncertain and that's when prices got crazy. There were potato inspectors approving or rejecting the Maine cargoes and

some of them were getting bribed and some of them were paid to say one thing when the other was true. The month of May was a period when a lot of the warehoused potatoes were also perishing. . . . It definitely made for an exciting, if corrupt, market.[27]

Traders from across the country and even Maine potato farmers were known to make the pilgrimage in May to New York to watch traders duke it out in the potato pits.

The old-school potato traders never would have guessed that the real threat on the horizon was an uneducated farmer from Boise, Idaho. Jack Richard Simplot was known as the "Idaho potato king," the nation's largest supplier and processor of potatoes. He even funneled millions of ready-cut french fries to McDonald's.[28] But Simplot was also known as a wheeler-dealer in the potato futures market. He first started making his fortune in onions, so much so that he once likened onion powder to gold dust.[29] However, when it became illegal to trade onions, Simplot parlayed his onion businesses into thirty thousand acres of land and started growing more potatoes. During World War II, one-third of all potatoes consumed by American GIs came from his land. By the late 1960s, he had become the largest supplier of potatoes to McDonald's and developed and shipped some of the first frozen potatoes. He even drove a car with the license plate "MR SPUD."[30]

But in the 1970s, he grew discontented; Simplot wanted Idaho, not Maine, to be the epicenter of the potato universe, and he saw the NYMEX traders as standing in his way. Because the NYMEX traders were accustomed to trading Maine potatoes, they had no interest in starting over in Idaho. On May 7, 1976, the May Maine potato–futures contract expired. While this was not unusual—the contract expired each year— traders on the floor could see that the outstanding short position for nearly two thousand potato contracts remained. This was very unusual, indeed: it meant the owners of those 1,911 contracts were still obligated to fulfill their promise. Simplot, betting against the NYMEX traders, had sold millions of dollars of potato futures, driving down prices in the process. But he didn't unwind his short bets before expiration, and he did not make good on them by delivering thousands of pounds of Maine potatoes.

When the final delivery deadline set by the exchange arrived at noon, 997 contracts still were unsettled, each representing 50,000 pounds of potatoes. Simplot didn't have any Maine potatoes to deliver. But he did have plenty of Idaho potatoes. He later conceded that he was "sucked in" by the market's upswings and sold a lot of contracts in the $19 to $16 range, but he did not try to buy back the contracts until much later. Contract trading stopped at $8.70, and he had missed his window, which left him scrambling for potatoes. Simplot tried to buy directly from Maine farmers with cash offers of $6.50 to $8. However, the farmers balked at his bid because they had received offers as high as $15 from export agents for their products.[31]

Simplot professed to be surprised by all the fuss, which *Time* magazine alternately called "The Great Potato Panic" and "The Great Potato Bust." He told a reporter: "There's nothing to get excited about. I think it will all work out."[32] The NYMEX might have begged to differ; the U.S. Commodity Futures Trading Commission banned the trading of potato futures indefinitely, effectively wiping out NYMEX's most prosperous business.[33] In the end, total estimated damage came to between $3 million and $5 million. Simplot was charged for attempting to manipulate the market. He was barred from commodities trading for six years and levied $50,000 in fines.[34]

Potatoes remain a footnote in American trading history. In 1996, the New York Cotton Exchange experimented with a short-lived potatoes contract. While still an active market in India, potatoes no longer trade in the United States—in Maine, Idaho, or otherwise.

Tomatoes

Tomato paste futures, launched on the Cotton Exchange in 1971, were a short-lived experiment. Though it seemed like a ripe and juicy opportunity, "it was too small; it never got off the ground," explains Joseph O'Neill, former president of the New York Cotton Exchange and former CEO of the exchange's Citrus Associates arm.

The problem? A lack of middlemen, O'Neill says. Most of the tomatoes went directly from a California co-op to a handful of tomato sauce makers, such as Del Monte and Ragu. "At the time, they didn't have a lot of merchants—the middlemen, like car dealers, who buy from the farmers and sell to the end users. Without a good trading base, it's never going to work." Although tomato paste met the storability requirement—as did tobacco and potato futures, which experienced an attempted revival in the 1980s—a paltry community of merchants to buy from growers and sell to end users diminished any need to trade futures on these products. And so tomato futures were a nonstarter.[35]

Orange Juice

The Cotton Exchange managed to find its stride with orange juice futures, a commodity that is still traded. In fact, this volatile, weather-driven futures market is among the most active in the world—perhaps not coincidentally, it is also one of the few markets with no major scandal to recount. For centuries, oranges and fresh orange juice were considered highly perishable, with a limited shelf life. The model for production and consumption of bottled orange juice was similar to fresh milk: it must be locally produced and locally consumed. Fresh oranges could be shipped longer distances to market, and then the fresh juice was squeezed by hand at home.

However, the citrus market changed radically when the process for making frozen concentrated orange juice (FCOJ) was invented in Florida, right after World War II. Thanks to the convenience factor (and encouraged further by a popular series of 1948 radio ads featuring Bing Crosby as a spokesperson for Minute Maid frozen orange juice concentrate),[36] consumers were quick to substitute FCOJ for fresh orange juice.

The more sophisticated storage and delivery methods meant that FCOJ had characteristics that made it suitable for futures trading: it could be created to consistent quality standards, and it was easy to store and deliver (initially, in large storage drums). The New York Cotton Exchange formed a Citrus Associates subsidiary, augmenting its existing contracts in cotton and wool, and it began trading FCOJ futures in 1966. At first, these contracts largely focused on Florida orange juice; as the OJ industry went global, and Brazil, in 2004, became the dominant citrus-producing region, the contract evolved into what is called the FCOJ-A contract, which also included orange juice from Brazil (and now juice from Costa Rica and Mexico as well). This remains the current benchmark contract.[37]

In 1979, the New York Cotton Exchange merged with the Coffee, Sugar, and Cocoa Exchange, creating the New York Board of Trade.[38] In 2006, the NYBOT came under the umbrella of the IntercontinentalExchange,[39] where FCOJ futures continue to trade, one of the last remaining produce-related contracts left in the United States.

Who can forget the role orange juice futures played in the plot of the 1983 film *Trading Places* (starring Dan Aykroyd and Eddie Murphy)? O'Neill fondly remembers the filming of the movie, which took place on the trading floor of the Cotton Exchange and was peopled with floor brokers from the NYMEX, from the COMEX (Commodity Exchange), from oils, and from metals, and "whoever wanted to come in and be in a movie." O'Neill, who says *Trading Places* is an accurate depiction of how the floor worked at the time, advised the filmmakers on, among other things, the prices used in the film: "They wouldn't happen in seven minutes, but they were real prices, from $0.30 to $1.50."[40]

What Trades Now

• *Frozen Concentrated Orange Juice*: Trades on the ICE. Contract size is 15,000 pounds (7 metric tons) of orange juice solids. U.S. grade A, or in trading shorthand, FCOJ-A. This is the world benchmark contract for the frozen concentrated orange juice market. Allowed countries of origin are Brazil (the largest supplier), the United States, Costa Rica, and Mexico. While FCOJ competes with NFC (Not From Concentrate) and reconstituted liquid juice, FCOJ is readily storable and easy to ship; it therefore remains the trading benchmark.

The strongest month for FCOJ typically is November, when traders are hedging against a freeze; the weakest month tends to be February, when traders are lifting those "freeze-protection" trades.[41]

• *Corn*: Trades on the CME. It is the only other fruit/vegetable product still actively traded in the United States (chapter 3).

Statue of Ceres, Roman goddess of grain, atop the Chicago Board of Trade, where soybean futures traded. (Image used with the permission of CME Group Inc. © 2011. All rights reserved.)

CHAPTER TEN

Super Soybeans

Those only who farm intensively will succeed with soy beans. The man who
grows two crops on the same ground at the same time, with one of them
weeds, should never try soy beans; better try cowpeas,
or better sell out and give all his time to politics.

OHIO FARMER, JANUARY 16, 1902

Now the number-two crop in America, the soybean, unbelievably, was
once the ugly duckling of the agricultural world, deemed fit for feeding
livestock but not people. Transitioning over the decades from "soja" to
"soya" to "soy," it is impossible now to imagine supermarkets devoid of
soybean-based products, from Tofutti ice cream to soy-based veggie bur-
gers. Nonvegetarians consume their share of soy too, whether in the form
of soybean oil, the most widely used edible oil in the United States, or via
soymeal fed to livestock. A growing global demand for nonfood soy-based
products—like ink, adhesives, some fabrics, and biodiesel—is equally important in the growth of soy. After corn, author Michael Pollan describes
soybeans as "the second leg supporting the industrial food system," fed to
livestock and now finding its way into two-thirds of all processed foods.[1] In
particular, soymeal is a key feed for poultry. Akin to the beef/corn futures
hedge, although broiler (chicken) futures no longer trade, some market
experts advise keeping an eye on the stock prices of publicly traded poultry
processors, such as Tyson Foods, as well as wholesale and retail prices for
chicken when soybean futures encounter volatility.

With so much at stake, it stands to reason that soybean futures are one
of the most active markets in the United States—second in crop production

as well as trading volume, both second only behind King Corn[2]—and traded widely on other bourses around the globe. And no wonder the soybean's by-product, soybean oil, was at the center of the 1960s debacle now known as the Great Salad Oil Swindle, considered by many to be one of the boldest acts of hubris and corruption in recent commodities history.

Soya Beans Get Their Start

Although soy seeds were introduced to the United States from Asia on a number of occasions throughout the nineteenth century, it was not until the end of the century that Americans would treat the plant as more than just a novelty.

That said, there certainly was a great deal of curiosity about the plant and its potential as both a food and an industry. One 1881 Clarksville, Texas, newspaper ad touted the "Soya Bean of Japan, Half Bean Half Pea" as "the richest human food known."[3] Another article, about "The Hairy Soja Bean," noted that it "forms a large part of the daily food of millions" in India, China, and Japan, although for Americans, the writer suggested that its "adaptability to fodder purposes" held great promise for soybeans "to become a valuable addition to the resources of the State."[4] Still another article, this one from a paper in Syracuse, New York, referenced a report read at the American Dairyman's Association meeting, held in town. Although the report suggests it would discuss the value of soy as cattle feed, instead it contains surprises about its food value in Japan and its potential in the United States: "It is there a leading article of diet, and is carried in the pockets of children and eaten as sweetmeats are here. Mr. H. Saze, the Japanese gentleman who read the paper, is a student in his senior year at Cornell University. He said the Soya bean has been cultivated for over twenty years by a seedsman in Marblehead, Mass., without any renewal of the seed by getting it from Japan."[5]

A number of wide-eyed accounts focused on how the soybean could be manipulated into other formats, through elaborate and seemingly mysterious means: "A vegetable meat of Japan, called 'torfu' [sic], is said to consist mainly of protein of the soya bean, and to be as nutritious and digestible as meat. It is sold in tablets, is white as snow, and tastes like fresh malt."[6] Read another account: "The Japanese have a mixture of the oil and the meal of the bean which they call 'miso,' a sort of butter, delicious and satisfying. Mixed and fermented with ground barley or wheat, there is made what is known as a chop soy, or chop-suey, a staple food, extremely popular with Orientals."[7]

Although the "soya bean" continued to be an object of interest, peanuts also were encroaching as a crop of interest in the late nineteenth century, particularly in the South, and one that Americans seemed to prefer as a potential food item, as opposed to the more foreign "soy." ("Soya" was streamlined to "soy" in the early 1920s, but "soy bean" remained two distinct words until the 1950s.) "The coming man in the South is the pea-vine farmer," crowed one Baltimore editorial.[8] Another article, running in the *Dallas Morning News*, suggested that the "oft-ridiculed peanut" might assume "great importance as a source of food." It not only renewed nutrients in the soil, the writer said, but also provided "the greatest amount of alimentation in the least volume and for the lowest price." Further, people just seemed to prefer the flavor and texture of peanuts far beyond soy and found them less mysterious to manipulate in recipes. The same *Morning News* article describes in minute detail how to boil peanuts to soften them for making a peanut butter–like puree and goes on to recommend peanuts in other preparations, ranging from "boiled with pork . . . superior to baked beans," or baked with salt into "a most toothsome cracker."[9] Although peanuts would not truly take hold in the American pantry until around 1900, when laborsaving equipment was invented for planting, cultivating, harvesting, and picking peanuts, looking back, it is surprising that peanuts did not edge out soybeans as the agricultural contract of choice. But farmers eagerly embraced both soy and peanuts as potential "money crops."

Cottonseed versus Soybeans

As late as the 1920s, soybeans were a minor crop with little commercial value. Farmers grew them—only to plow the bean plants under to restore nutrients to cornfields. Soybean oil, used primarily in industry, was imported from China. But what solidified soy in the agricultural pantheon was the near-decimation of the cotton crop in the early twentieth century. Cotton crops—used, among other things, to produce cottonseed oil— were ravaged by a boll weevil epidemic around the turn of the century.

Cottonseed oil was widely used in the paint industry and other areas, and it yielded important components: oil and meal, for feeding cattle and fertilizing fields. Without cottonseed oil, farmers and others needed to scramble for an alternative, and therefore soybean oil assumed greater importance. J. W. Allison, chairman of the Bureau of Publicity for the Texas Cotton Seed Crushers' Association, declared the soya bean "a dangerous rival to cotton seed products," but grudgingly noted its superior oil yield compared with cottonseed.[10] The United Kingdom was the first to switch cattle feed from cottonseed cake to soybean cake; Germany was anticipated to be next. When Denmark, "for a long time the best customers of the United States for cotton seed cake,"[11] switched to soybean cake for feeding cattle, U.S. farmers and oil producers grew downright mournful. Also, it was not a small detail that huge tanks of "Manchurian soya bean" oil and meal were imported duty-free, surely setting off further alarm bells among American farmers and businessmen (import duties would finally be imposed in 1921).

Soybeans were big business, but they weren't yet food. Occasionally, news items ran about scientific breakthroughs that yielded early iterations of soy milk. But "soya-milk," "soya-cheese," and the like were generally objects of incredulity and derision. "They're going to make milk from the soya bean, and eggs by a chemical trick; and cobless corn made of nitrogen they'll serve with a chickenless chick," jeered *Harper's Weekly*.[12]

Wartime Provisions

As many foods became scarce during wartime, suddenly soybeans became a lauded food item. During both world wars, the government prodded Americans to grow—and eat—soybeans. Among other measures, during World War I, the government implored farmers to grow more wheat and other food, for consumption at home as well as for export to Europe. The fed encouraged an increase in the production of soybeans and peanuts "in order to supplement beans and peas as human food, as a source of much needed oil, and as animal feed."[13]

Mandated wheatless and meatless days brought "soy loaf" into the American vocabulary, and soy flour was one of the seventeen recognized substitutes for standard wheat flour that could be employed to bake "victory bread." Recipes for various soy-spiked foods ran in newspapers, whether intended as helpful hints or wartime rationing propaganda. One typical example:

> Soy-bean muffins—To make muffins from soy-bean flour, take about one-half cup of soy flour, about one and one-half teacupfuls of wheat flour, one-half teaspoonful salt, two eggs, one teacupful of sweet milk, two rounded teaspoonfuls of baking powder and one and one-half table-spoonfuls of melted but not hot butter. Beat well together, adding the melted butter last, and bake in gem pans in a hot oven. This will make about 12 muffins.[14]

When wartime receded into the distance, Americans quickly returned to other protein sources, but U.S. farmers continued to cultivate soybean crops, which retained value as animal feed and as a source of oil for use in paints and varnishes, soaps, and other personal items. By the 1930s, and as far afield as California, farmers began to question the wisdom of importing soy. After all, it grew easily in American soil and required less rainfall compared with wheat and corn crops. Also, the industrial possibilities for soy were being further realized. Soy caught the attention of automotive giant Henry Ford, who, during the Depression, looked for ways to help American farmers by finding manufacturing uses for agricultural products. From 1932 to 1933 alone, scientists in Ford's employ spent more than $1 million on soy research.[15] This and later work helped improve on a number of old products and create some new ones—many intended for automotive use, such as soy plastics for automobile parts, soy shock-absorber fluid, and soy-based paint for automobiles—as well as others meant for consumption, such as soy meat substitutes and soy coffee. Many of these surprising items were displayed at the 1933–1934 Chicago World's Fair (Century of Progress) in the Ford-sponsored Industrialized American Barn, where Ford invited reporters to a lunch and dinner featuring dozens of soy foods, including soybean cheese, soybean crackers, soy milk, and soy ice cream.

In 1941, Ford built his famed "Soybean Car," with exterior plastic panels made from soy, to exhibit at the Dearborn Days festival in Michigan. (Ford's use of soy in the manufacture of vehicles stimulated soy farming in the state.)[16] Although the outbreak of World War II suspended all auto production, including the soybean-plastic experiment, the 1930s saw notable advances in soy processing, utilization, financing, and research, driven in part by Ford's efforts. The Midwest in particular became a booster of the soybean plant (and not coincidentally, the Chicago Merc was the first to trade futures on the product).[17]

World War II fueled a massive expansion of the U.S. soybean industry as supplies of coconut oil and other edible fats dried up. According to the American Soybean Association, U.S. soybean production nearly tripled between 1940 and 1946, from 78 million to 201 million bushels. During the war, soy was used in glue to hold U.S. torpedo boats together; as a foam stabilizer in U.S. Navy fire extinguishers (soy protein has "marvelous fire-fighting properties," the USDA raved); in K rations; in pork sausage; in macaroni for the U.S. Army; and in the domestically consumed margarine that became a common substitute for increasingly scarce butter and lard.[18]

As the end of the war grew near, Americans once again pushed soy away from the table, frustrating U.S. growers who had become successful at producing soy crops. Luckily, export markets absorbed the soy supplies. Political changes and postwar economic problems prevented China from restoring its prewar soybean exports to Europe, and U.S. soy producers eagerly filled the gap. By 1949, the United States was exporting 23 million bushels of soybeans. Ironically, Japan and Germany were two of the earliest international markets for U.S. soybeans and continue to be very important customers. By 1969, for the first time, soy was exported in the form of soybeans or soybean meal in an amount equal to more than half the crop itself.[19]

Illinois became the center of soybean and soybean oil production, and acreage devoted to growing soybeans increased "at wildfire pace." One bushel of soybeans yielded a gallon of oil, and that oil was described as a "jack of all trades," acceptable for use in paints and varnishes in place of linseed oil. Some observers speculated that "within ten years the soy bean industry will rival in size and importance the cotton industry in the south"—a bold statement for the time. But by the 1970s, American farmers uprooted rows of cotton to plant row upon row of soybean plants in their place. Indeed, at soy's peak in the 1970s, U.S. farmers supplied four-fifths of the world soybean trade.[20]

Also aiding the industry were three new food trends. First was the increase in U.S. consumption of traditional Asian soy foods. The Kikkoman Corporation noticed in the 1950s and 1960s that Americans began eating more often in Asian restaurants. American military men who were part of the Japanese occupation after World War II and who served in Korea came back with a taste for Asian food. By 1972, Kikkoman had decided to build a factory in Walworth, Wisconsin, the "first significant Japanese manufacturing facility ever built in the United States," and still the largest soy sauce plant in the Western world.[21]

Second—and to soy farmers, far more important—industrialized nations began consuming more meat, notably chicken, but also beef and pork. This extended meat binge, coupled with advances in the conversion of soymeal into animal feed, caused demand for soy to shoot upward. In fact, meal evolved into the industry's number-one revenue producer because a bushel of beans yields more than four times as much meal as oil. The eventual importance of the poultry industry to the soy market is illustrated by statistics from the 1990s, when chickens consumed significantly more soy protein in America than anyone else, some 40 percent of the yearly supply.[22]

The third food trend is the advent of soy oil. During wartime, the product's undesirable flavor and short shelf life forced manufacturers to limit its proportion in margarine to no more than 30 percent. But as its flavor improved, soy oil in the United States began to be used much more often in liquid form as a home-cooking or salad oil.[23] Now, it is the most widely used cooking oil in the United States, accounting for more than 75 percent of total U.S. consumer vegetable fat and oil consumption.[24] Together, these three changes in the American diet helped turn soy into the "money crop" that farmers had envisioned in the late nineteenth century.

Trading in the "Bean Pit"

Chicago, naturally, became the financial center of the soybean universe. In October 1936, soybean futures began trading on the CBOT, joining wheat, corn, oats, rye, barley, and cotton. The first lot (5,000 bushels) sold at a rate of $1.20 a bushel, the *Chicago Daily Tribune* reported. Other contracts followed. In 1940, the Memphis Cotton Exchange in Tennessee inaugurated "the world's only futures market for soybean meal." Ten years later, the CBOT introduced soybean oil futures. After World War II, soybean oil was finally getting its due as a food-grade commodity and product to trade on a global scale. "Trading in soybean oil will start at a time when production of cottonseed oil, the main competitor of bean oil, will be reduced about one-third compared with a year ago because of plans for less planting of cotton," the *Chicago Daily Tribune* explained. "Bean oil is regarded as the most versatile of the vegetable fats, with use in paints, salad and cooking oils, and soaps as well as margarine."[25]

An exporter of soybean oil would use futures to protect against price increases between the time an order was received and when it would be delivered to a foreign port. Meanwhile, a domestic oil processor might use the same contract to hedge during the time it would take to process oil into shortening or margarine, protecting against potential price declines.

By 1963, roughly thirty years after the debut of the soybean future, the contract traded in the "bean pit" was credited for immense strides in trading volume on the CBOT. The exchange said that by the bushel, soybeans accounted for more trade than the other commodities combined. The soybean trades that were handled covered more than 5 billion bushels, compared with nearly 2 billion for corn, 325 million for oats, and 252 million for rye.[26] The soybean was profitable, and it was here to stay.

The Great Salad Oil Swindle

Not unlike the grain market corners of the 1800s or the onion-trading stink of the 1950s, the soybean market had its share of shady characters who sought to exploit the market for untoward financial gain. And in the early 1960s, that character was Anthony "Tino" De Angelis, the self-described "King of Salad Oil." Writer Norman Miller, who reported on the salad oil case for the *Wall Street Journal*, describes De Angelis as deceptively "unimpressive" in appearance: "His bland moon face dissolved into a series of chins which gobbled up his fat neck. Black horn-rimmed glasses framed thick graying hair, combed straight back. . . . Put an apron and a chef's cap on him and he would have looked right baking pizza, deadpan in the window of a little Italian restaurant."[27] Yet De Angelis was the brains behind the Great Salad Oil Swindle, which ultimately bankrupted twenty banks and commodities and securities firms, including an American Express unit, and caused losses in the hundreds of millions of dollars.

Interestingly, the Salad Oil Swindle, later characterized by *Time* magazine as "the most prodigious swindle in modern times," almost went unnoticed by the general public, overshadowed by the shocking news of the assassination of President John F. Kennedy on November 2, 1963. But in commodities circles, some traders still cringe at the mention of Tino De Angelis.

In 1955, De Angelis organized Allied Crude Vegetable Oil Refining Corporation, headquartered in the grimy port section of Bayonne, New Jersey, "just a thirty-five minute drive in Tino's Cadillac to the money markets of Wall Street."[28] Allied was heavily involved in shipping foodstuffs between the United States and Europe in the years following World War II, particularly soybean oil and cottonseed oil used to make salad dressings, referred to collectively as "salad oil." By the late 1950s, Allied was supplying more than 75 percent of the edible oils shipped overseas.[29] De Angelis gained notoriety for shipping both substandard and uninspected vegetable oil to government contractors and then overcharging them. Oddly, his shady record did him little harm in the business world. Many seemed to regard De Angelis, as summed up by one banker's description, as "extremely resourceful."[30] "He had a knack for making money and this was really all that counted," Miller summarizes. "As long as the profits rolled in, the eminently respectable businessmen who dealt with De Angelis were willing to overlook anything."[31]

Adding to the existing mix of investors, a subsidiary of consumer credit giant American Express, called American Express Field Warehousing, agreed to act as Allied's custodian. At the time, this business—issuing warehouse receipts as collateral for bank loans—was fairly commonplace. This appealed to De Angelis because American Express would vouch for the goods of clients that stored inventory in its warehouses. Clients could then use American Express's warehouse receipts to take out loans, in this case secured by the value of the salad oil inventory. De Angelis became one of American Express's first big clients in 1957.[32]

The brazen shenanigans that followed are now legendary. When a ship loaded with salad oil would arrive in the docks, inspectors would test the product and confirm the ship was carrying salad oil. In actuality, there was little salad oil in evidence. The company would fill salad oil tanks with seawater and float a few feet of oil on top. This is the oil the inspectors would test. Of course, everyone assumed the tanks were brimming with salad oil. The company used a maze of interconnecting pipes to transfer oil to different tanks. Hoodwinked inspectors did their jobs and were taken out to lunch. Special compartments and even tanks filled with gasoline were used to fool warehouse representatives and others who came to check the inventories. De Angelis's close-knit group became expert at hiding the fact that the tanks contained mostly seawater.[33]

The fraudulent "salad oil" piled up in the warehouse while De Angelis, undaunted, devised a daring check-kiting swindle. A cloak-and-dagger act of switching checks among a local New Jersey bank, a large New York bank, and Bunge Corporation—a sizable vegetable exporter—was part of the furious underhanded activity taking place.[34] After the "dazzling" check passing, Allied was home free with warehouse receipts for real oil it could use as it pleased, Bunge officials later testified.[35] According to some accounts, the amount of those warehouse receipts far exceeded all the oil there could possibly be in the country.

De Angelis used much of those millions to speculate in cottonseed and soybean oil futures, which eventually led to his downfall. With a pad of stolen American Express Warehouse receipts in his desk, De Angelis was flooding Wall Street with a stream of forged receipts to support his "beserk" buying of futures contracts.[36] His speculation became wilder and wilder, all stemming from his asserted confidence that big foreign sales were about to materialize. Once his long-future position reached alarming heights, it was impossible to stop without the house of cards crashing down—De Angelis either personally or through companies he controlled held 40 percent of the total soybean oil futures contracts outstanding on the CBOT and nearly 85 percent of the cottonseed oil contracts on the New York Produce Exchange.[37] The bubble expanded, enveloping more banks, brokers, exporters, and others, until it finally burst in November 1963, when De Angelis filed for bankruptcy, for both himself and Allied. American Express was left to foot the bill on the bad loans, and the search for the salad oil began. In total, the fraudulent inventory represented more than 1.8 billion pounds in faked soybean and cottonseed oil, with a stated value of $175 million.[38] Panic hit when investors learned there was nothing to support the loans. People swarmed over to Bayonne—and the truth dawned that hardly any of the oil existed. Not only were most of the tanks filled with seawater, sludge, or acidulous oils but some of the tanks couldn't even be located. The investors' money and the salad oil were never recovered.

Smarting from the scandal, the Produce Exchange began losing business. "We've survived the Civil War, the First World War, the Great Depression, and World War I," griped an anonymous veteran member on the exchange floor. "But the present mess shapes up as the exchange's worst commercial crisis."[39] The Produce Exchange halted cottonseed oil—at the time, one of its two most actively traded products[40]—"until further notice."[41] Meanwhile, in 1963, the Chicago Board of Trade introduced cottonseed oil futures. Although the Produce Exchange later tried to revive cottonseed oil trading, it was too late, and the contract eventually was shuttered for good. This was considered by many to be the final nail in the coffin for the New York Produce Exchange. In order to survive, the Produce Exchange had to undergo an identity change. It became the International Commercial Exchange in 1970, under the sponsorship of the New York Produce Exchange, which was then subsumed under this new entity. Although the scandal may have been the death knell for the Produce Exchange, it did not mean the end of soybean futures. Short-term volatility ensued in the soybean oil market—which was hard to separate from the general financial turmoil in the markets following the Kennedy assassination. Decades later, soybean oil remains an active market today.

What happened to De Angelis? Famously taciturn, even in court (confronted with inventory sheets showing there had once been 800 million pounds of oil in American Express's now nearly empty tanks, De Angelis merely deadpanned, "You show me a piece of paper, but I know not from where it comes"), in 1965, he was convicted and spent seven years in prison. De Angelis never learned his lesson. In the late 1970s, he returned to prison for three years following a Ponzi scheme that defrauded Indianapolis pig farmers. In 1992, at the age of seventy-seven, he was again arrested, this time for allegedly swindling $1 million in pork products from a Toronto-based meat company.[42]

What Trades Now

- *Soybeans*: Trades on the CME. Contract size is 5,000 bushels (127 metric tons). A "mini-size" soybean futures contract also exists, at 1,000 bushels (25 metric tons).[43] Primary uses for soybeans include livestock feed and edible oil. Soybean is one of the most popular oilseeds in the world; the oil is an edible commodity but also used in the manufacture of plastics, solvents, and other industrial products. Soybean oil trades as its own commodity.

- *Soybean Meal*: Trades on the CME. Contract size is 100 tons. Soybean meal is the dominant protein supplement used in livestock and poultry feeds.[44]
- *Soybean Oil*: Trades on the CME. Contract size is 60,000 pounds (27 metric tons).[45] As the main ingredient in a wide range of cooking products, soybean oil is the most widely used edible oil in the United States. It accounts for 80 percent of margarine production and for more than 75 percent of total U.S. consumer vegetable fat and oil consumption.[46] Soybean oil is the primary component of biofuel, an increasingly important alternative energy source.
- *Crude Palm Oil*: Trades on the CME. Contract size is 50,000 pounds (25 metric tons). The underlying product is Malaysian crude palm oil, the world's most consumed edible oil, and trades actively in Singapore. This is a "cash-settled" contract (no physical delivery of the underlying product), and trades for speculative and hedging purposes.[47]

"How come there's no Peking Duck Exchange?" asks one of a series of magazine advertisements run by the Chicago Mercantile Exchange (early 1970s). (Courtesy of Ryan Carlson)

CHAPTER ELEVEN

The Future of Food Futures?

Contracts to Consider

Under my watch, we tried several other contracts [besides pork bellies].
We tried a shrimp market—I wanted to get away from meats,
but it didn't work. We tried turkey—it worked for a little while.
We also tried broilers and hams. Ninety out of a one hundred fail,
but when you hit the jackpot, it's worth it.
LEO MELAMED, FORMER CHAIRMAN OF THE CHICAGO MERCANTILE EXCHANGE

Pardon the pun, but this chapter is intended largely as food for thought. None of the food products discussed here are represented on U.S. commodities exchanges. However, there is reasonable evidence that a market could be made for each of them—or at least, that an *argument* for a market could be made, which is almost as good. All these commodities are considered to be sufficiently important that either the USDA or the Commodity Research Bureau Commodity Yearbook (or both) regularly provide pricing data for them. And experts regularly consider this pricing data in their analyses and predictions. Some products, such as canola oil and olive oil, trade on other exchanges around the world. But none of them are currently traded in the United States. At least . . . not yet.

Canola (Rapeseed)

Canola—a contraction of "Canada oil"—is a genetic variation of rapeseed (a member of the mustard family) that was developed by Canadian plant breeders specifically for its nutritional qualities and its low level of saturated fat. Canola oil is used as a salad oil, cooking oil, and for margarine, as well as in the manufacture of inks, biodegradable greases, pharmaceuticals, fuel, soap, and cosmetics. It is also the world's third-largest source of vegetable oil, behind soybean oil and palm oil.[1]

For four thousand years, the oil from the rapeseed was used in China and India for cooking and as lamp oil—not surprisingly, rapeseed also trades today on China's Zhengzhou Commodity Exchange. But ICE Futures Canada is the primary market for canola futures, even though approximately 70 percent of Canada's canola oil is exported to the United States.[2] This certainly argues for U.S.-based trade in canola futures.

Cassava

Could one of the next great global contracts be the humble cassava? Also called manioc, mandioca, and yuca, this starchy drought-resistant root vegetable is a major source of dietary energy for more than 500 million people, particularly in developing countries. Cassava is the primary source of tapioca, but it is also eaten raw or boiled and processed into livestock feed, starch and glucose, and flour, as well as used in pharmaceuticals. One species of cassava has been successfully grown for its rubber.[3]

However, cassava is likely off the radar screen for American traders because the United States is not among the top cassava producers or importers/exporters. The world's largest producers are Nigeria and Thailand; the largest exporters Thailand and Vietnam; and the two main importers China and the Republic of Korea.[4]

Fish

With the exception of frozen shrimp on Japan's Kansai Commodities Exchange, no one is trading fish or seafood in the futures marts. But it wasn't always that way—shrimp previously was widely traded, including in Chicago, and fishmeal (used primarily for animal feed) was a standard U.S. contract. But now? It is not traded, even though fish is the primary source of protein for a large portion of the world's population and global demand is on the rise.

Given the obvious demand as well as various supply issues (all of the world's major fishing areas have either reached or exceeded their limits), this seems like a ripe market for the type of volatility upon which traders thrive. Although salmon springs readily to mind as a high value–broad demand variety suitable for trading, the Fisheries Statistics Division of the U.S. Department of Commerce lists ten key commercial species contributing the most to total U.S. revenue: American lobster, blue crab, menhaden, Pacific halibut, Pacific salmon, sablefish, sea scallops, shrimp, tuna, and walleye pollack.[5] Would salmon or lobster futures be viable, or a derivative instrument combining the most popular finfish and shellfish prices? It is certainly something to consider.

Grapes or Grape Juice Concentrate

Worldwide, more than 430 million tons of fruit is produced each year. Here in the United States, the most widely produced fruit (according to the USDA) is the orange, and it is represented in the commodities sphere in the form of frozen concentrated orange juice futures. The next most produced fruit is the apple; it has traded in the past and may soon trade again, in the form of apple juice–concentrate contracts (for more on both of these, see chapter 9). But what about the third-ranked fruit—grapes? In addition to the juice and flavorings industries, think also about grapes' most fun by-product, wine, which has its own form of futures market. And there could be viability to a grape juice–concentrate contract at some point down the road.

Honey

Sugar has long edged out honey in the global marketplace, which could be one reason honey does not trade as a futures contract. The closest thing to a U.S. spot price is the National Honey Board's monthly compilation of honey retail and wholesale prices, using data from *Bee Culture* magazine, and import bulk prices, using data from the U.S. Department of Commerce. For those seeking more detailed information, the USDA produces a *National Honey Report* each month. This report notes colony, plant, and market conditions in the major U.S. states and regions. Also, it lays out U.S. exports and imports of honey by country, quantity, and value.[6] If you are a honey producer wondering how much Extra Light Amber Honey the United States imported from Argentina last month, the *Honey Report* is your go-to source.

Olive Oil

Although many Americans cook with olive oil as much as, if not more than, they do with soybean oil or butter, olive oil does not trade on the U.S. exchanges. Instead, it trades on the Mercado de Futuros del Aceite de Oliva (MFAO; translated as "Olive Oil Futures Market") in Jaén, Spain. The city of Jaén, part of Andalusia, is known as the world capital of olive oil because it is the biggest producer of this "liquid gold," as the locals refer to it.

Initially created in 2004 to provide a mechanism for olive oil producers to protect themselves against price swings, the bourse includes producers, cooperatives, and olive oil mills, although, in some years, as much as 50 percent of trading volume has been attributed to a combination of olive oil bottlers and players in the financial and industrial sectors.[7]

By the end of 2010, the MFAO had negotiated 190,085 contracts (an average of 760 contracts daily), up from 143,335 in 2009, and the cash value of production traded in 2010 was about €330 million ($468.7 million).[8] The MFAO had expressed ambitions for international expansion, specifically to Portugal and Italy.

Salt

It is baffling that salt is an essential element in the human diet, a key seasoning around the world, and an important food preservative—yet it has never traded as a commodity, even though pepper has. The regions of ancient Ethiopia and Tibet appreciated salt's value: it served as money in the form of cakes there. Further, the United States is a key producer as well as consumer of salt. Although America is no longer the number-one producer of salt—as of 2005, China is—the United States continues to be a solid number two and exports much of that salt to Canada. Of course, some might argue whether a salt contract would be salient as a food-based commodity; the chemical industry consumes 40 percent of total salt sales, with much of that destined for feedstock. Salt for highway de-icing accounts for another 38 percent of U.S. demand. By comparison, the food industry accounts for a paltry 4 percent of domestic salt consumption.[9]

Sheep and Lambs

Futures for sheep, which are raised for both their wool and their meat, traded for a while in London and Australia but no longer do today. It is likely no coincidence that production levels have declined in New Zealand and Australia, but that has been counteracted by a substantial increase in China.[10] Perhaps we'll see sheep futures on China's exchanges one day.

And how about in the United States? Although we are not among the top sheep producers in the world, America still has a thriving sheep- and lamb-farming industry, and the USDA reports on sheep and lamb prices as well as farm value. Although sheep futures are not yet traded in the United States, if David Anderson has his way, that could change in coming years. Anderson, a professor of economics at Texas A&M University, is among those leading the charge for Livestock Risk Protection for lamb prices, shorthanded as LRP-Lamb. In 2007, a pilot project for the price-protected product was launched.

"A national representative price was needed," explained Anderson in 2008, shortly after the pilot program launched. "Local prices are sometimes not reported due to a lack of sales and more seasonal markets. Local conditions may vary widely across the country so that one local market does not reflect another local market. . . . LRP-Lamb is not dependent on a single market, method of sale, or single LRP-Lamb contract week. Overall, LRP-Lamb does provide price risk-management protection against unexpected declines in national prices or the overall lamb market."[11] Although the LRP-Lamb project seems unlikely to provide the hedging mechanism of a large and formal commodities exchange, it certainly appears to be helpful for providing price discovery, another key function of exchanges.

Tea

Coffee is a highly active commodity—so why not tea? Half the world's population drinks tea; it is the world's most popular beverage next to water. In 1883, an ancillary tea exchange, called the Importers' and Grocers' Exchange, was organized near the Coffee Exchange in New York, but it closed less than two years later.[12] Perhaps it is time to bring the tea exchange back, in a more global capacity. It is primarily produced in Asia (China is the largest producer, followed by India and Sri Lanka) but consumed in Europe (Russia and the United Kingdom are the largest tea importers, by a large margin).[13]

The idea that we could trade these commodities may seem far-fetched, but I assure you it is not. In fact, I can offer as evidence shortlists of products that have been considered for trade—most of which never came to be (again, at least not yet). In 1969, on the drawing board were plans for the formation of a Pacific Coast Commodity Exchange, which was to open in 1971 with coconut oil as its first contract. It never came to fruition—a shame considering the other products that were to be added for trade, including California wines, raisins, tomato paste, tuna, and crabmeat, as well as nonfood items, such as cultured pearls and Pacific currencies from Japan, Taiwan, the Philippines, and Australia.[14] In addition, the former Chicago Mercantile Exchange's New Commodities Committee has, at various times, considered the following as possibilities for futures contracts: canned hams, carcass beef, coconut oil, corn oil, cranberries, cucumbers, dehydrated alfalfa, dried milk, frozen spare ribs, frozen strawberries, grapes, honey, lard, mushrooms, olive oil, peanut oil, pepper, pork loins, rice, safflower oil, Scotch whisky, sheep, tomato juice, tomato paste, and wine.[15] It is a potentially rich and vast bounty that leads right back to my original assessment of the first commodities contracts: together they read like a menu. In fact, with all the potential past and future contracts that abound, I would conclude that there is more than enough to make up a virtual meal—there is plenty to offer as a fabulous aperitif, dessert, and surplus for stocking pantries everywhere.

APPENDIX
Food Commodities Traded on Non-U.S. Exchanges

Like the United States, most countries around the world use exchanges to hedge the prices of agricultural commodities. I present here a list of selected non-U.S. commodities, and where they trade, compiled from the 2011 *CRB Commodity Yearbook*, published by the Commodity Research Bureau, plus additional listings provided by the various exchanges. Please note that the list is not intended to be comprehensive (though it is certainly thorough), and that some products may have ceased trading or exchanges may have merged or otherwise changed since this list was compiled. Further, the exchanges name and spell the products as they see fit, so nomenclature may vary (i.e., "US Soybeans" versus "American Soybeans").

That said, it is fascinating to see where products trade, and what this says about global foodways. In some cases, it speaks volumes about which foods are valued enough to trade where they do—for example, India's cardamom, coriander, and turmeric markets, or adzuki (red beans), traded only in Japan. In other cases, historians can cast an eye toward the products that no longer trade in America but live on elsewhere, such as the European Processing Potatoes market on Eurex in Frankfurt, Germany, and eggs, on the Central Japan Commodity Exchange. And in yet another sense, consider which products have such global and universal value that they trade across virtually every geographic area. Notably, sugar, soybeans, and wheat, in all its various forms, are represented most widely.

CONTRACT	EXCHANGE
Arabica Coffee	Bolsa de Mercadorias & Futuros, Brazil
Corn	Bolsa de Mercadorias & Futuros, Brazil
Live Cattle	Bolsa de Mercadorias & Futuros, Brazil
Soybeans	Bolsa de Mercadorias & Futuros, Brazil
Euro Wheat	Budapest Stock Exchange, Hungary
Feed Barley	Budapest Stock Exchange, Hungary
Feed Corn	Budapest Stock Exchange, Hungary
Feed Wheat	Budapest Stock Exchange, Hungary
Mill Wheat	Budapest Stock Exchange, Hungary
Rapeseed	Budapest Stock Exchange, Hungary
Sunflower Seed	Budapest Stock Exchange, Hungary
Hen Egg	Central Japan Commodity Exchange

Butter	Eurex, Frankfurt, Germany
European Processing Potatoes	Eurex, Frankfurt, Germany
Hogs	Eurex, Frankfurt, Germany
Piglets	Eurex, Frankfurt, Germany
Skimmed Milk Powder	Eurex, Frankfurt, Germany
Canola (Rapeseed)	ICE Futures Canada
Western Barley	ICE Futures Canada
Corn	JSE Securities Exchange of South Africa
Sorghum	JSE Securities Exchange of South Africa
Soybeans	JSE Securities Exchange of South Africa
Sunflower Seeds	JSE Securities Exchange of South Africa
Wheat	JSE Securities Exchange of South Africa
White Maize	JSE Securities Exchange of South Africa
Yellow Maize	JSE Securities Exchange of South Africa
Corn	Kansai Commodities Exchange, Japan
Frozen Shrimp	Kansai Commodities Exchange, Japan
Raw Sugar	Kansai Commodities Exchange, Japan
Red Beans	Kansai Commodities Exchange, Japan
US Soybeans	Kansai Commodities Exchange, Japan
Crude Palm Oil	Malaysia Derivatives Exchange
Corn	Mercado a Término de Buenos Aires, Argentina
Sorghum	Mercado a Término de Buenos Aires, Argentina
Soybeans	Mercado a Término de Buenos Aires, Argentina
Sunflower	Mercado a Término de Buenos Aires, Argentina
Wheat	Mercado a Término de Buenos Aires, Argentina
Raw Rice	Moscow Interbank Currency Exchange, Russia
Rice Groats	Moscow Interbank Currency Exchange, Russia
Almond	Multi Commodity Exchange of India
Barley	Multi Commodity Exchange of India
Cardamom	Multi Commodity Exchange of India
Coriander	Multi Commodity Exchange of India
Crude Palm Oil	Multi Commodity Exchange of India

Guar Seed	Multi Commodity Exchange of India
Kapasia Khalli (Cottonseed Oil)	Multi Commodity Exchange of India
Melted Menthol Flakes	Multi Commodity Exchange of India
Mentha Oil	Multi Commodity Exchange of India
Potato (Agra)	Multi Commodity Exchange of India
Potato (Tarkeshwar)	Multi Commodity Exchange of India
Refined Soya Oil	Multi Commodity Exchange of India
Soya Bean	Multi Commodity Exchange of India
Sugar M	Multi Commodity Exchange of India
Turmeric	Multi Commodity Exchange of India
Wheat	Multi Commodity Exchange of India
Barley	National Commodity & Derivatives Exchange, India
Chana (chickpea)	National Commodity & Derivatives Exchange, India
Chilli (chile)	National Commodity & Derivatives Exchange, India
Coriander	National Commodity & Derivatives Exchange, India
Jeera (cumin)	National Commodity & Derivatives Exchange, India
Mustard Seed	National Commodity & Derivatives Exchange, India
Pepper (black pepper)	National Commodity & Derivatives Exchange, India
Turmeric	National Commodity & Derivatives Exchange, India
Wheat	National Commodity & Derivatives Exchange, India
Corn	NYSE Liffe Paris
Malted Barley	NYSE Liffe Paris
Rapeseed	NYSE Liffe Paris
Skimmed Milk Powder	NYSE Liffe Paris
Wheat No. 2	NYSE Liffe Paris
Cocoa No. 7	NYSE Liffe United Kingdom
Robusta Coffee	NYSE Liffe United Kingdom
Wheat	NYSE Liffe United Kingdom
White Sugar	NYSE Liffe United Kingdom
Corn	Rosario Futures Exchange, Argentina

Soybeans	Rosario Futures Exchange, Argentina
Wheat	Rosario Futures Exchange, Argentina
Refined Sugar	Russian Trading Systems Stock Exchange
Sugar	Russian Trading Systems Stock Exchange
Robusta Coffee	Singapore Commodity Exchange
MLA/SFE Cattle	Sydney Futures Exchange, Australia
American Soybeans	Tokyo Grain Exchange, Japan
Arabic Coffee	Tokyo Grain Exchange, Japan
Azuki (Red Beans)	Tokyo Grain Exchange, Japan
Corn	Tokyo Grain Exchange, Japan
Non-GMO Soybeans	Tokyo Grain Exchange, Japan
Raw Sugar	Tokyo Grain Exchange, Japan
Robusta Coffee	Tokyo Grain Exchange, Japan
Wheat	Turkish Derivatives Exchange, Turkey
Early Rice	Zhengzhou Commodity Exchange, China
Hard White Winter Wheat	Zhengzhou Commodity Exchange, China
Rapeseed Oil	Zhengzhou Commodity Exchange, China
Strong Gluten Wheat	Zhengzhou Commodity Exchange, China
White Sugar	Zhengzhou Commodity Exchange, China

Epilogue

The commodities market has come a long way from those first grain trades at Haine's Feed Store in Chicago. The exchanges have grown, evolved, and consolidated into the monoliths we know today. Meanwhile, a number of commodities contracts have come and gone. Just as food traditions evolve, so do food commodities.

Why have so many of these contracts disappeared into history? In some cases, the culprit is technology. For example, egg futures languished as agricultural advancements meant year-round egg laying. And improvements in refrigeration and distribution eliminated the remaining vestiges of seasonality in eggs. The lack of seasonality smoothed out the volatility that makes it necessary (and lucrative) to hedge by trading futures contracts. More recently, pork belly contracts have vanished, as technological improvements in pork processing mean there is no longer a need to trade futures in this product. Other times, the problem is simple human greed. Might onions or salad oil futures still be trading today if scandals had not harassed government officials into throwing up their hands and regulating those contracts out of existence?

As some contracts are eased out, what can we expect regarding new futures? While it is difficult to peer into the future, it seems certain that contracts traded in the United States are likely to reflect *global* food needs and availabilities—not just those of American eaters. Just as the markets for soybeans has flourished as global populations consume soybeans in any number of forms, next up might be the fledgling apple juice concentrate market—a product increasingly made and consumed outside of the United States. Think also about where populations are flourishing and consumer demand (and capital) is accelerating. Corporations are very much thinking this way—and just as Starbucks and McDonald's are pushing to open outlets in China in the coming years, expect speculators to be placing their bets right alongside those corporate giants in the coffee and beef futures markets.

Speaking of global perspectives, while this book focuses on U.S. bourses, it is impossible not to consider the degree to which marketplaces in the United States now are linked with those in other countries. Derivatives markets trade on a global playing field. The CME Group and ICE proudly trumpet their global partnerships on their landing pages, and digital enhancements mean it is possible—some would argue necessary—to trade soybeans or coffee across multiple platforms and countries. Headspinningly complicated instruments have been devised by experts with the intent of maximizing profits on the spreads between various contracts. It is not such a far leap to wonder whether, after all the consolidation in the markets, a fully global marketplace, trading fully global food-based futures contracts, might be an option in the not-so-distant future.

But in the meantime, Americans continue to rely on the agricultural futures market to aid in "price discovery" and steadiness—trading keeps food prices generally consistent and at reasonable levels. Farmers, food processors and manufacturers, importers and exporters, retailers, restaurateurs, and consumers are all reliant, to some degree, on the futures market for ultimately getting food on the table.

However, some critics argue loudly that the pendulum has swung too far in the other direction, blaming rampant speculation for driving inflation and causing a disconnect between the commodities markets and real food prices. "Excessive speculation drives up spot prices," Murray Worthy of the World Development Movement scolds during a televised debate. "Futures markets are directly linked to spot prices and therefore what people pay for food."[1] Howard Schultz, chief executive of the Starbucks coffee chain, is another voice of dissent, lashing out at "hedge funds, index funds and other ways to manipulate the market" for spiking coffee prices.[2] One grain trader on the exchange floor even notably complains that the influx of "outside money" from in-and-out speculators changed the Chicago exchange into a "casino" and introduced a "Wall Street mentality" into the commodities markets.[3] Opponents to this view say it is difficult to pinpoint evidence because the financialization of commodities trading became a major factor roughly at the same time as demand for physical commodities from emerging economies started to increase rapidly.

In the end, regulators agree, at least in part, that excessive speculation played a role in driving up food and gas prices. In October 2011, the Commodity Futures Trading Commission voted 3 to 2 to approve a federal rule to cap trading in commodities futures. The cap on futures contracts, which goes into effect in 2012, restricts the volume of futures contracts that financial investors can trade for agricultural contracts and twenty-seven other commodities, including energy and precious-metals contracts. Under the rule, agriculture companies themselves are exempt from the cap. Some say the rule does not go nearly far enough in protecting food prices.

One fact is clear: the commodities markets and food prices are linked more closely than ever before. A United Nations report shows that money invested in food commodities shot up from $13 billion in 2003 to $260 billion just five years later.[4] Why do so many investors want to put their cash into the commodities market, anyway? Frankly, the biggest bullish factor for food prices is simply strong demand. Food demand is growing, not only because of a rising global population but also because of an increase in better living standards in the developing world. More people can afford to buy greater quantities of better-quality food. As people gain more household income, they typically move up the protein scale and eat more meat and dairy products, which in turn requires more grain and feed to support greater livestock production. The United Nations predicts that three-quarters of the growth in food demand in the past decade has come from the emerging markets.

The problem of high food prices is not likely to go away anytime soon, experts agree. The UN predicts that food output will have to increase by an extraordinary 70 percent by 2050, as the world population grows to

9 billion people from 6.6 billion at present. And as food supply and demand shifts, expect financial investment related to food commodities to shift accordingly.

Availability and affordability of food are critical inputs in how everyone decides what to buy and where to buy it. Although it may not be apparent on the surface, the commodities market and food prices—and therefore, what we eat—are linked in important, pervasive, and symbiotic ways.

Notes

Introduction

1. Richard Wheatly, "The New York Produce Exchange," *Harper's New Monthly Magazine*, July 1886.

1. How Does Commodities Trading Work?

1. Chad Hart, interview with author, August 17, 2011.
2. Michael Pollan, *The Omnivore's Dilemma: A Natural History of Four Meals* (New York: Penguin Press, 2006), 59. Pollan credits the original account of "the invention of agricultural commodities" to William Cronon, *Nature's Metropolis: Chicago and the Great West* (New York: Norton, 1991).
3. Pollan, *Omnivore's Dilemma*, 59.
4. Alan Bush, interview with author, August 17, 2011.
5. Ibid.
6. Bill G. Lapp, interview with author, August 15, 2011.
7. Ibid.
8. Ibid.
9. Hart interview.
10. Ibid.

11. Ibid.

12. Ibid.

2. The Spice Route

1. John Keay, *The Spice Route: A History* (Berkeley: University of California Press, 2006), 21.

2. Jack Turner, *Spice: The History of a Temptation* (New York: Vintage Books, 2005), 58.

3. "Apicius," Encyclopaedia Romana, University of Chicago, http://penelope .uchicago.edu/~grout/encyclopaedia_romana/wine/apicius.html (accessed May 22, 2012).

4. Ibid.

5. Apicius, *Cooking and Dining in Imperial Rome*, ed. Joseph Dommers Vehling, August 19, 2009, http://www.gutenberg.org/files/29728/29728-h/29728-h .htm#bki_chxiii (accessed August 16, 2011), 45, 54.

6. M. T. Khan, *Spices in Indian Economy* (Delhi: Academic Foundation, 1990), 28.

7. Keay, *Spice Route*, 28–29.

8. Henry Hobhouse, *Seeds of Change: Five Plants That Transformed Mankind* (New York: Harper & Row, 1985), xi.

9. Keay, *Spice Route*, 108.

10. Ibid., 214.

11. Ibid., 233.

12. Khan, *Spices in Indian Economy*, 249–251.

13. "To Trade Pepper Futures," *New York Times*, June 9, 1937.

14. "Along Wall Street," *New York Times*, June 13, 1937.

15. "Pepper Market Expands," *New York Times*, July 23, 1937.

16. "Pepper Trading Resumed in New York," *Wall Street Journal*, December 3, 1946.

17. "N.Y. Produce Exchange to Resume Trading in Black Pepper Futures," *New York Times*, April 2, 1960.

18. Michael Benson, "Black Pepper Prices Soar Under Squeeze," *New York Times*, July 3, 1960.

19. Ibid.

20. Stephen Josefik and Stanley W. Penn, "Grand Old Lady's Grief," *Wall Street Journal*, December 9, 1963.

21. *Coffee, Tea, Cocoa, and Spices*, prepared by the Food Division, Office of Industry and Commerce, Bureau of the Census (Washington, D.C., 1947–1950).

22. *2011 CRB Commodity Yearbook* (Chicago: Commodity Research Bureau, 2011).

23. R. W. Apple Jr., "Following the Pepper Grinder All the Way to Its Source," *New York Times*, October 29, 2003.

24. Ajayan, "Deserted by Trade, World's Oldest Pepper Exchange Going to Seed," *Livemint*, January 16, 2008, http://www.livemint.com/2008/01/16231549/ Deserted-by-trade-world8217.html (accessed March 7, 2011).

25. Khan, *Spices in Indian Economy*, 47.

26. "About Us," National Commodity & Derivatives Exchange, http://www .ncdex.com/AboutUs/Profile.aspx (accessed March 7, 2011).

3. The Commodity That Built a Nation

1. Michael Pollan, *The Omnivore's Dilemma: A Natural History of Four Meals* (New York: Penguin Press, 2006).

2. *2011 CRB Commodity Yearbook* (Chicago: Commodity Research Bureau, 2011). Data for 2010 is the most recent available.

3. Pollan, *Omnivore's Dilemma*, 26.

4. Arturo Warman, *Corn and Capitalism: How a Botanical Bastard Grew to Global Dominance* (Chapel Hill: University of North Carolina Press, 2003), 179.

5. Ibid., 108–109.

6. Ibid., 111.

7. Ibid., 117.

8. Ibid., 118.

9. Ibid., 122.

10. Betty Fussell, *The Story of Corn* (New York: Knopf, 1992), 19.

11. "The New York Grain Trade," *Working Farmer*, January 1, 1861.

12. The envelope, estimated to date to 1861, shows a graphic printed in purple ink of a man carrying sheaves of corn stalks, with the words: "Corn (Not cotton.) is King." It is at the American Antiquarian Society, Worcester, Mass.

13. "The Corn Show at Paris," *American Agriculturist*, March 1889.

14. Warman, *Corn and Capitalism*, 161.

15. Ibid., 160.

16. "A Visit to the States: The Metropolis of the Lakes," *Times* (London), October 21 and 24, 1887.

17. Quoted in William Cronon, *Nature's Metropolis: Chicago and the Great West* (New York: Norton, 1991), 226.

18. Warman, *Corn and Capitalism*, 175.

19. Eugene Brooks, *The Story of Corn and the Westward Migration* (Chicago: Rand-McNally, 1916).

20. Warman, *Corn and Capitalism*, 180–181.

21. Ibid., 181.

22. "Grain Trade Wins Place in Annals of 1917," *Chicago Daily Tribune*, December 31, 1917.

23. "Corn Deposes Wheat as Ruler of Chicago Board of Trade Pits," *Chicago Daily Tribune*, January 8, 1931.

24. Pollan, *Omnivore's Dilemma*.

25. Warman, *Corn and Capitalism*, 184.

26. Ibid., 187.

27. Dan Morgan, *Merchants of Grain* (New York: Penguin Books, 1980), 142.

28. Pollan, *Omnivore's Dilemma*, 39.

29. Ibid., 58–59.

30. Ibid., 63.

31. Ibid., 66.

32. Ibid., 86.

33. Ibid., 89.

34. Ibid., 103.

35. "Sweet Competition: New Corn Derivative Challenges Big Sugar as a Shake-Out Looms," *Wall Street Journal*, November 2, 1976.

36. "Minneapolis Exchange to Trade Syrup Futures," *Wall Street Journal*, March 11, 1987.

37. Sarahelen Thompson, Philip Garcia, and Lynne Dallafior Wildman, "The Demise of the High Fructose Corn Syrup Futures Contract: A Case Study," *Journal of Futures Markets* 16, no. 6 (1996): 697–724.

38. "Grain and Oilseed Futures and Options," CME Group, http://www.cmegroup.com/trading/agricultural/files/AC-268_Grains_FC_FINAL_SR.pdf (accessed April 27, 2012).

39. "Distillers' Dried Grain Futures," CME Group, http://www.cmegroup.com/trading/agricultural/files/AC-398_DDGS_FC_r6.pdf (accessed April 27, 2012).

4. Great Grains

1. "History of Chicago: The Illinois and Michigan Canal," *Chicago Magazine: The West as It Is* 1, no. 5 (1857): 389.

2. William Cronon, *Nature's Metropolis: Chicago and the Great West* (New York: Norton, 1991), 65–66.

3. Ibid., 67.

4. Ibid., 76.

5. David Greising and Laurie Morse, *Brokers, Bagmen, and Moles: Fraud and Corruption in the Chicago Futures Markets* (New York: Wiley, 1991), 45.

6. Christopher Prior Willeard, *Farming Futures: A Guide to Agricultural Commodity Futures Markets* (Cambridge: Woodhead-Faulkner, 1984), 9.

7. Ibid., 10.

8. Quoted in Cronon, *Nature's Metropolis*, 146.

9. Ibid., 115.

10. Quoted in ibid., 116.

11. *American Elevator and Grain Trade*, January 15, 1894.

12. William G. Ferris, *The Grain Traders: The Story of the Chicago Board of Trade* (East Lansing: Michigan State University Press, 1988), 19.

13. Alfred T. Andreas, *History of Chicago from the Earliest Period to the Present Time*, vol. 2, *1884–1886* (Chicago: Andreas, 1884), 362.

14. P. G. Smith, "The World's Food Exchange," *Donahoe's Magazine*, January–June 1905.

15. Ibid.

16. Ibid.

17. Emily Lambert, *The Futures: The Rise of the Speculator and the Origins of the World's Biggest Markets* (New York: Basic Books, 2011), 10–11.

18. Dan Morgan, *Merchants of Grain* (New York: Penguin Books, 1980), 97.

19. Greising and Morse, *Brokers, Bagmen, and Moles*, 50–53.

20. Ferris, *Grain Traders*, 118.

21. Ibid., 128.

22. Quoted in Greising and Morse, *Brokers, Bagmen, and Moles*, 53–54.

23. Allen B. Paul, "The Past and Future of the Commodities Exchanges," *Agricultural History* 56, no. 1 (1982): 292.

24. Greising and Morse, *Brokers, Bagmen, and Moles*, 78–79.

25. Walter Thornbury and Edward Walford, *Old and New London: The City Ancient and Modern* (London: Cassell, 1881), 179.

26. Trading Organizations Filings Database, U.S. Commodity Futures Trading Commission, http://sirt.cftc.gov/SIRT/SIRT.aspx?Topic=TradingOrganizations&implicit=true&type=DCM&CustomColumnDisplay=TTTTTTTT (accessed April 27, 2012); Paul, "Past and Future of the Commodities Exchanges," 287–305.

27. Paul, "Past and Future of the Commodities Exchanges," 291–292.

28. "50 Years of Futures," Futures Industry Association, http://www.futuresindustry.org/50-years-of-futures.asp (accessed February 8, 2011).

29. Ruthie Ackerman, "CBOT Holders Choose to Merge with CME," *Forbes*, July 9, 2007, http://www.forbes.com/2007/07/09/cbot-cme-closer-markets-equity-cx_ra_0709markets40.html (accessed June 27, 2011).

30. "Grain and Oilseed Futures and Options," CME Group, http://www.cmegroup.com/trading/agricultural/files/AC-268_Grains_FC_FINAL_SR.pdf (accessed April 30, 2012).

31. Ibid.

32. Ibid.

33. Kansas City Board of Trade, http://www.kcbt.com/contract_wheat.html (accessed April 30, 2012).

34. Minneapolis Grain Exchange, http://www.mgex.com/contract_specs.html (accessed April 30, 2012).

5. Butter-and-Egg Men

1. Edward Wiest, "The Butter Industry in the United States: An Economic Study of Butter and Margarine" (Ph.D. diss., Columbia University, 1916), 146–147.

2. Michael Shapiro, "Ruling the Roost," *Smithsonian*, July 2003.

3. Douglas Martin, "TriBeCa Dairy Wholesaler Is Link with Pushcart Past," *New York Times*, September 27, 1996.

4. Bob Tamarkin, *The Merc: The Emergence of a Global Financial Powerhouse* (New York: Harper Business, 1993), 27–35. See also http://www.wisconsinhistory.org/wmh/pdf/wmh_autumn01_strey.pdf.

5. "Ode to Chicago's New Mercantile Exchange," *Chicago Daily News*, October 1919.

6. H. S. Irwin, *Evolution of Futures Trading* (Madison, Wis.: Mimir, 1954), 18. Aside from this reference, I have not seen "limed egg" or "pickled egg" quotations listed or discussed elsewhere.

7. Emily Lambert, *The Futures: The Rise of the Speculator and the Origins of the World's Biggest Markets* (New York: Basic Books, 2011), 28–29.

8. Quoted in "Poor Old Public Must Eat Fresh Butter and Eggs," *Chicago Daily Tribune*, January 14, 1919.

9. "Butter and Egg Board Prohibits Sale of Futures," *Chicago Daily Tribune*, June 2, 1917.

10. David Greising and Laurie Morse, *Brokers, Bagmen, and Moles: Fraud and Corruption in the Chicago Futures Markets* (New York: Wiley, 1991), 76.

11. "Butter and Egg Men Hard B'iled," *Los Angeles Times*, March 18, 1926.

12. Susan Abbott Gidel, "100 Years of Futures Trading: From Domestic Agricultural to World Financial," *Futures Industry Magazine*, December 1999–January 2000, http://www.futuresindustry.org/fi-magazine-home.asp?a=607 (accessed February 10, 2011).

13. Joseph Egelhof, "U.S. Back in Old Familiar Role of Buying Eggs," *Chicago Daily Tribune*, December 12, 1949.

14. Quoted in Greising and Morse, *Brokers, Bagmen, and Moles*, 82.

15. Tamarkin, *Merc*, 157.

16. Ibid., 168–172.

17. Ibid., 245.

18. "Dairy Futures and Options," CME Group, http://www.cmegroup.com/trading/agricultural/files/AC-194_Dairy_Fact_Card.pdf (accessed April 30, 2012).

19. Ibid.

20. Ibid.

21. Ibid.

22. Ibid.

23. "Cash-Settled Cheese Futures and Options," CME Group, http://www.cmegroup.com/trading/agricultural/files/AC-421_Cheese-Futures-Options-Fact-Card-05.10.pdf (accessed April 30, 2012).

6. The Mochaccino Market

1. IntercontinentalExchange employee, interview with author, February 3, 2011.

2. Quoted in David Brandon, *Life in a Seventeenth Century Coffee Shop* (Stroud, Eng.: Sutton, 2007).

3. Mark Pendergrast, *Uncommon Grounds: The History of Coffee and How It Transformed Our World* (New York: Basic Books, 1999), 13.

4. Brandon, *Life in a Seventeenth Century Coffee Shop*.

5. "Business and the Coffee House," *Bulletin of the Business Historical Society* 2, no. 3 (1928): 10–13.

6. Ibid.

7. Pendergrast, *Uncommon Grounds*, 46.

8. Ibid., 52.

9. Ibid., 61–62.

10. Ibid., 64–66.

11. Ibid., 66.

12. Abram Wakeman, *History and Reminiscences of Lower Wall Street and Vicinity* (New York: Spice Mill, 1914).

13. "Hilarious Coffee Brokers Fined," *New York Times*, December 18, 1884.

14. Wakeman, *History and Reminiscences*.

15. Cyrus Townsend Brady, *The Corner in Coffee* (New York: Dillingham, 1904).

16. Sidney W. Mintz, *Sweetness and Power: The Place of Sugar in Modern History* (New York: Viking Penguin, 1986), 185.

17. Elizabeth Abbott, *Sugar: A Bittersweet History* (New York: Overlook Press, 2010), 25.

18. Ibid., 280.

19. Ibid., 295–296.

20. Ibid., 279.

21. *Formation of the Exchange* (New York: New York Coffee and Sugar Exchange, 1957), 6.

22. Nortz and Company, *Coffee and Sugar Facts* (New York: New York Coffee and Sugar Exchange, 1924), 3.

23. *2011 CRB Commodity Yearbook* (Chicago: Commodity Research Bureau, 2011).

24. *The History and Operation of the New York Coffee and Sugar Exchange, 1882–1952* (New York: New York Coffee and Sugar Exchange, 1952).

25. "Cocoa Exchange Growth Rapid," *Wall Street Journal*, May 10, 1929.

26. "Gay Urges Cooperation Among Exchanges to Meet Problems," *Wall Street Journal*, October 2, 1935.

27. Maria Shao, "Listless New York Cocoa Exchange Plans a Smaller Contract in Quest for Business," *Wall Street Journal*, August 17, 1978.

28. Cocoa Futures/Product Specifications, IntercontinentalExchange, https://www.theice.com/productguide/ProductSpec.shtml?specId=7 (accessed April 30, 2012).

29. Coffee C Futures/Product Specifications, IntercontinentalExchange, https://www.theice.com/productguide/ProductSpec.shtml?specId=15 (accessed April 30, 2012).

30. Robusta Futures/Product Specifications, IntercontinentalExchange, https://www.theice.com/productguide/ProductSpec.shtml?specId=738 (accessed April 20, 2012).

31. Sugar No. 11 Futures/Product Specifications, IntercontinentalExchange, https://www.theice.com/productguide/ProductSpec.shtml?specId=23 (accessed April 30, 2012).

32. *2011 CRB Commodity Yearbook*, 321.

33. IntercontinentalExchange employee interview.

34. Sugar No. 16 Futures/Product Specifications, IntercontinentalExchange, https://www.theice.com/productguide/ProductSpec.shtml?specId=914 (accessed April 30, 2012).

35. IntercontinentalExchange employee interview.

7. Cattle Call

1. Betty Fussell, *Raising Steaks: The Life and Times of American Beef* (Orlando, Fla.: Harcourt, 2008), 18–22.

2. "The Cattle Trade of New York," *The Plough, the Loom, and the Anvil*, July 1848.

3. "Statistics of Agriculture: New York Cattle Trade for 1853," *Merchants' Magazine and Commercial Review*, June 1, 1854.

4. Ibid.

5. Jeremy Rifkin, *Beyond Beef: The Rise and Fall of the Cattle Culture* (New York: Dutton, 1992), 61.

6. Ibid., 88.

7. John Clay, *My Life on the Range* (Chicago: privately published, 1924).

8. Rifkin, *Beyond Beef*, 88.

9. Ibid., 95.

10. Ibid., 89–90.

11. Ibid., 93.

12. Ibid., 94.

13. Ibid., 96.

14. Ibid.

15. "Inspection and Grading of Meat and Poultry: What Are the Differences?" U.S. Department of Agriculture, Food Safety and Inspection Service, http://www.fsis.usda.gov/Factsheets/Inspection_&_Grading/index.asp (accessed May 1, 2012).

16. Fussell, *Raising Steaks*, 22–23.

17. William Cronon, *Nature's Metropolis: Chicago and the Great West* (New York: Norton, 1991), 216.

18. Ibid., 218–224.

19. Joseph G. McCoy, *Historic Sketches of the Cattle Trade of the West and Southwest* (1874; repr., Ann Arbor, Mich.: University Microfilms, 1966), 40.

20. Rifkin, *Beyond Beef*, 70.

21. Fussell, *Raising Steaks*, 23–24.

22. Rifkin, *Beyond Beef*, 115.

23. Upton Sinclair, *The Jungle* (New York: Doubleday, 1906), 114.

24. Emily Lambert, *The Futures: The Rise of the Speculator and the Origins of the World's Biggest Markets* (New York: Basic Books, 2011), 58.

25. Henry Harrison Bakken, ed., *Futures Trading in Livestock: Origins and Concepts* (Madison, Wis.: Mimir, 1970).

26. Bob Tamarkin, *The Merc: The Emergence of a Global Financial Powerhouse* (New York: Harper Business, 1993), 134.

27. Leo Melamed, *For Crying Out Loud: From Open Outcry to the Electronic Screen* (New York: Wiley, 2009), 13.

28. Quoted in Tamarkin, *Merc*, 129.

29. David Greising and Laurie Morse, *Brokers, Bagmen, and Moles: Fraud and Corruption in the Chicago Futures Markets* (New York: Wiley, 1991), 84–85.

30. Rishaad Salamat, Andrea Tan, and Michael Wei, "McDonald's to Open a Restaurant a Day in China in Four Years," *Bloomberg News*, July 29, 2011, http://www.bloomberg.com/news/2011-07-29/mcdonald-s-franchises-to-account-for-up-to-20-of-china-business.html (accessed August 6, 2011).

31. *2011 CRB Commodity Yearbook* (Chicago: Commodity Research Bureau, 2011).

32. Feeder Cattle Futures/Contract Specifications, CME Group, http://www.cmegroup.com/trading/agricultural/livestock/feeder-cattle_contract_specifications.html (accessed May 1, 2012).

33. Live Cattle Futures/Contract Specifications, CME Group, http://www.cmegroup.com/trading/agricultural/livestock/live-cattle_contract_specifications.html (accessed May 1, 2012).

8. This Little Piggy Made a Market

1. Scott Kilman, "Latest Diet Fad Helps Put Hog Farmers in Fat City," *Wall Street Journal*, October 19, 2004.

2. William Cronon, *Nature's Metropolis: Chicago and the Great West* (New York: Norton, 1991), 225.

3. Ibid., 228–229.

4. Frederick Law Olmsted, *A Journey Through Texas: Or, A Saddle-Trip on the Southwestern Frontier* (1857; repr., Austin: University of Texas Press, 1978), 9.

5. "The Pork Trade of the West: Cincinnati the Great Pork Market," *New-York Daily Times*, December 4, 1852.

6. Cronon, *Nature's Metropolis*, 229.

7. Ibid., 230.

8. Quoted in Carl Sandburg, "Making the City Efficient," *La Follette's*, September 30, 1911.

9. Cronon, *Nature's Metropolis*, 209.

10. Jack Wing, *The Great Union Stock Yards of Chicago* (Chicago: Religio-Philosophical Publishing Association, 1865), 11.

11. Cronon, *Nature's Metropolis*, 210.

12. Ibid., 208.

13. Wing, *Great Union Stock Yards of Chicago*, 15–19.

14. Ibid., 24.

15. Cronon, *Nature's Metropolis*, 211–212.

16. Upton Sinclair, *The Jungle* (New York: Doubleday, 1906), 41.

17. Cronon, *Nature's Metropolis*, 124.

18. Bob Tamarkin, *The Merc: The Emergence of a Global Financial Powerhouse* (New York: Harper Business, 1993), 99.

19. Leo Melamed, interview with author, December 11, 2006.

20. Ibid.

21. "Mart Rounds Out Diet," *New York Times*, August 24, 1961.

22. Melamed interview.

23. Thomas W. Ennis, "Trading in Futures of Pork Bellies Is Begun Here," *New York Times*, December 2, 1971.

24. Michael Pollan, *The Omnivore's Dilemma: A Natural History of Four Meals* (New York: Penguin Press, 2006), 51.

25. Edward Lee, "Meat Shortage Disrupts Futures Trading," *Chicago Tribune*, August 2, 1973.

26. Geoffrey Keating, "One Big, Noisy Gamble," *Chicago Tribune*, November 4, 1973.

27. Kilman, "Latest Diet Fad."

28. William L. Hamilton, "Luxury Cut, Surprise Source," *New York Times*, April 25, 2001.

29. As evidenced, for example, by the publication of Fergus Henderson, *Nose to Tail Eating: A Kind of British Cooking* (London: Pan Macmillan, 1999).

30. The rich layer of fat is described as "Nature's Icing" in Julia Moskin, "A Futures Market in Flavor: Pork Bellies Are Just the Start," *New York Times*, May 7, 2003.

31. Jennifer McLagan, *Fat: An Appreciation of a Misunderstood Ingredient* (New York: Ten Speed Press, 2008).

32. Amanda Hesser, "Challenging Chefs with Odd Cuts," *New York Times*, January 29, 2003.

33. Carolyn Cui and Theopolis Waters, "Pork Bellies Now 'Nontrading Places,'" *Wall Street Journal*, December 27, 2010.

34. Ron Plain, interview with author, January 2011.

35. Ibid.

36. Jim Robb, interview with author, January 2011.

37. Lean Hogs Futures/Contract Specifications, CME Group, http://www.cme group.com/trading/agricultural/livestock/lean-hogs_contract_specifications.html (accessed May 1, 2012).

9. When Money Grows on Trees

1. E. R. Carhart, "The New York Produce Exchange," *Annals of the American Academy of Political and Social Science* 38, no. 2 (1911): 211–214.

2. George Auerbach, "Old Produce Market Was Never Like This," *New York Times*, November 22, 1959.

3. "The New York Produce Exchange: Wide Scope of Its Operations and History of Its Growth," *New York Times*, September 22, 1901.

4. Sidney Hoos, "Futures Trading in Perishable Agricultural Commodities," *Journal of Marketing* 6, no. 4 (1942): 359.

5. John Houseman, *Run-Through: A Memoir* (New York: Simon and Schuster, 1972), 53.

6. David Greising and Laurie Morse, *Brokers, Bagmen, and Moles: Fraud and Corruption in the Chicago Futures Markets* (New York: Wiley, 1991), 73–75.

7. Confirmed by representative of CME Group, November 11, 2011.

8. Elizabeth M. Fowler, "Apple Futures Contracts Make Their Debut," *New York Times*, August 5, 1969.

9. Minneapolis Grain Exchange, http://www.mgex.com/ajc (accessed April 25, 2011).

10. Bob Tamarkin, *The Merc: The Emergence of a Global Financial Powerhouse* (New York: Harper Business, 1993), 18.

11. Greising and Morse, *Brokers, Bagmen, and Moles*, 79.

12. Ibid.

13. Ibid.

14. Ibid., 79–80.

15. Ibid., 80.

16. Ibid., 81.

17. Alan Bush, interview with author, August 17, 2011.

18. Greising and Morse, *Brokers, Bagmen, and Moles*, 81.

19. Ibid.

20. Ibid., 81–82.

21. Quoted in Tamarkin, *Merc*, 103.

22. Ibid., 104.

23. Greising and Morse, *Brokers, Bagmen, and Moles*, 80–82.

24. "Commodities: The Great Potato Bust," *Time*, June 7, 1976.

25. Leah McGrath Goodman, *The Asylum: The Renegades Who Hijacked the World's Oil Market* (New York: HarperCollins, 2011), 39.

26. Ibid., 39–40.

27. Quoted in ibid., 40.

28. "Great Potato Bust."

29. Goodman, *Asylum*, 46.

30. Ibid., 47.

31. "Great Potato Bust."

32. Quoted in ibid.

33. Goodman, *Asylum*, 52.

34. Simplot died in 2008, but the J. R. Simplot Company remains one of the largest privately held international food-processing and agricultural companies in the world—supplying potatoes and other food products to the food service industry around the world.

35. Joseph O'Neill, interview with author, March 17, 2011.

36. "Bing Crosby to Go on Air for Vacuum Foods," *Wall Street Journal*, October 7, 1948. It is also worth noting that Crosby owned twenty thousand shares of Vacuum Foods, Minute Maid's parent company. The *WSJ* reported that this was a new arrangement—the first time an entertainer owned stock in a company whose product he was advertising.

37. "Frozen Concentrated Orange Juice," IntercontinentalExchange, https://www.theice.com/publicdocs/ICE_FCOJ_Brochure.pdf (accessed May 2, 2012).

38. "New York Board of Trade Historic Timeline," New York Board of Trade, 2004.

39. "IntercontinentalExchange Enters into Agreement to Acquire New York Board of Trade," IntercontinentalExchange press release, September 14, 2006, http://ir.theice.com/releasedetail.cfm?ReleaseID=237339 (accessed May 2, 2012).

40. O'Neill interview.

41. "Frozen Concentrated Orange Juice."

10. Super Soybeans

1. Michael Pollan, *The Omnivore's Dilemma: A Natural History of Four Meals* (New York: Penguin Press, 2006), 35.

2. *2011 CRB Commodity Yearbook* (Chicago: Commodity Research Bureau, 2011), 248.

3. Advertisement, *Standard* (Clarksville, Tex.), March 25, 1881.

4. "The Hairy Soja Bean," *San Francisco Bulletin*, January 25, 1882.

5. T. D. Curtis, "Agriculture: Current Agricultural Topics," *Northern Christian Advocate*, March 2, 1882.

6. "Ten Minutes in Science: What Is Being Done in the Field of Invention and Discovery," *Sioux City Journal*, June 16, 1896.

7. "Soy Bean Competes with Cotton Seed Meal," *Dallas Morning News*, April 18, 1909.

8. "The Coming Man in the South," *Sun* (Baltimore), June 15, 1893.

9. "The Peanut as a Food," *Dallas Morning News*, April 25, 1894.

10. "Raises the Soya Bean on a Farm Near Ennis," *Dallas Morning News*, July 14, 1909.

11. "Danes Have Deserted Cotton Seed Cakes," *Lexington (Ky.) Herald*, January 3, 1910.

12. "Food of the Future," *Harper's Weekly*, reprinted in *Dallas Morning News*, April 27, 1913.

13. Arthur Sears Henning, "More Wheat! Nation's Plea to the Farmer," *Chicago Daily Tribune*, February 19, 1918.

14. "Use of Soy Bean Flour for Bread Is Suggested," *Morning Oregonian* (Portland), April 18, 1915.

15. Christine M. Du Bois, Chee-Beng Tan, and Sidney Mintz, *The World of Soy* (Urbana: University of Illinois Press, 2008), 214.

16. Ibid.

17. Ibid., 213.

18. Ibid., 215.

19. American Soybean Association, http://www.soygrowers.com/soyindustry/destined.htm (accessed July 5, 2011).

20. "U.S. Losing Share of World Trade," *Wall Street Journal*, December 3, 1992.

21. Du Bois, Tan, and Mintz, *World of Soy*, 217.

22. Ibid., 217–218.

23. Ibid., 219.

24. *2011 CRB Commodity Yearbook*, 243.

25. "Futures Trade in Soybean Oil Begins Monday," *Chicago Daily Tribune*, July 13, 1950.

26. "Sidelights: Soybeans Fatten Futures Trade," *New York Times*, July 20, 1963.

27. Norman C. Miller, *The Great Salad Oil Swindle* (New York: Coward McCann, 1965), 7.

28. Ibid., 18.

29. Ibid., 20.

30. Ibid., 29.

31. Ibid., 32.

32. Ibid., 74.

33. Ibid., 79–83, 92.

34. Ibid., 124.

35. Ibid., 125.

36. Ibid., 145.

37. Stephen Josefik and Stanley W. Penn, "Grand Old Lady's Grief," *Wall Street Journal*, December 9, 1963.

38. Miller, *Great Salad Oil Swindle*, 179.

39. Quoted in Josefik and Penn, "Grand Old Lady's Grief."

40. According to Joseph O'Neill, fishmeal was the other most actively traded product on the New York Produce Exchange at the time.

41. Richard Phalon, "The Great Vegetable-Oil Mystery," *New York Times*, November 15, 1964.

42. William Power, "Who's Back in Jail? It's Tino De Angelis, for the Third Time," *Wall Street Journal*, December 24, 1992.

43. "Grain and Oilseed Futures and Options," CME Group, http://www.cmegroup.com/trading/agricultural/files/AC-268_Grains_FC_FINAL_SR.pdf (accessed May 3, 2012).

44. Ibid.

45. Ibid.

46. 2011 *CRB Commodity Yearbook*, 243.

47. Crude Palm Oil Futures/Contract Specifications, CME Group, http://www.cmegroup.com/trading/agricultural/grain-and-oilseed/crude-palm-oil-futures_contract_specifications.html (accessed May 3, 2012).

11. The Future of Food Futures?

1. 2011 *CRB Commodity Yearbook* (Chicago: Commodity Research Bureau, 2011), 17.

2. Ibid.

3. Ibid., 20.

4. Ibid.

5. "Fisheries Economics of the United States 2009," U.S. Department of Commerce, National Oceanic and Atmospheric Administration, May 2011, http://www

.st.nmfs.noaa.gov/st5/publication/econ/2009/FEUS%202009%20ALL.pdf (accessed April 14, 2012).

6. National Honey Board/Honey Industry Resources, http://www.honey.com/nhb/industry/industry-statistics (accessed May 4, 2012).

7. Julie Butler, "Stagnant Prices, Uncertainty Take Toll on Olive Oil Futures," *Olive Oil Times*, May 24, 2011, http://www.oliveoiltimes.com/olive-oil-business/europe/olive-oil-futures/15950 (accessed November 7, 2011).

8. Ibid.

9. "Salt," U.S. Geological Survey, Mineral Commodity Summaries, January 2011, http://minerals.usgs.gov/minerals/pubs/commodity/salt/mcs-2011-salt.pdf (accessed April 14, 2012).

10. *2011 CRB Commodity Yearbook*, 231.

11. David P. Anderson, "Q&A: Market Prices and LRP-Lamb," American Sheep Industry Association, November 1, 2008, http://www.sheepusa.org/?page=site/text&nav_id=ae8c6a16f610a3bcd45440e545e2a9e1 (accessed April 14, 2012).

12. Abram Wakeman, *History and Reminiscences of Lower Wall Street and Vicinity* (New York: Spice Mill, 1914), 163.

13. *2011 CRB Commodity Yearbook*, 278.

14. Bob Tamarkin, *The Merc: The Emergence of a Global Financial Powerhouse* (New York: Harper Business, 1993), 424.

15. Ibid., 425.

Epilogue

1. *Street Signs*, CNBC, January 7, 2011.

2. Jack Farchy, "Starbucks Decries Speculators as Coffee Prices Spike," *Financial Times*, May 26, 2011.

3. "Price Formation in Financialized Commodity Markets," United Nations Conference on Trade and Development, June 2011, http://www.unctad.org/en/docs/gds2011_en.pdf (accessed April 16, 2012).

4. "The State of Food Insecurity in the World 2011," Food and Agriculture Organization of the United Nations, http://www.fao.org/docrep/014/i2330e/i2330e.pdf (accessed April 16, 2012).

Index

Italic page numbers indicate material in tables or figures.

trading instruments, grain elevator receipts as, 47
Trading Places (Duke), 123
Trading Places movie, 136
Tribeca neighborhood, 63–64, 70
Trinidad, 85
Trotter, Charlie, 119
trusts, 56–57
turkey futures, 91
turmeric, 24
Tyson Foods, 139

uncured bacon, 116
Union Pacific railroad, 96
Union Stock Yard, 114
Union Stockyards (Chicago), 90, 98
United Kingdom, 20, 21; "beef-eaters of Europe," 93–96; and purchase of U.S. land and cattle, 95; repeal of Corn Laws, 46; switch from cottonseed to soybean cake, 142; tea trade and, 80; "to-arrive" contracts in, 46; wheat imports from California, 54–55; and "whole beast" movement, 119
United States: 1884 anti-"alien holdings" sentiment, 95; 1930s drought, 43; 1972 grain sales to Russia, 117; beef exports, 33, 93–94, 100; coffee imports in, 80–81; corn belt, 33–34; mass transportation, 32; salt exports, 156; sheep and lambs, 157; spice market in, 21–23; sugar beets, 84; westward expansion, 32, 45, 93, 111; wheat exports during Crimean War, 48
Uruguay, 35
USDA (U.S. Department of Agriculture), 12; beef grades, 95; *Corn Show* at Paris Exposition, 30–31; crop reports, 12; "New York Spot Prices," 23; WWI shutdown of wheat futures, 69
U.S. Food Products Corporation, 57

U.S. Industrial Alcohol Company, 57
U.S. Industrial Chemicals, 57

Venezuela, 85
"victory bread," 142
Vietnam, 154
volatility, 10, 131, 163

Wakeman, Abram, 82
Wall Street, 92, 108
"Wall Street mentality," 165
Wan Tong Trading Company, 23
Ward, Anthony, 86
warehouse receipts, 57, 147–148
Warman, Arturo, 28, 29, 34
War of 1812, 80
wartime rationing, 22
WD-50, 119
West Africa, 85
wheat, 29; 1888 corner, 50–51; CBOT "wheat pit," 50; Crimean War European demand, 48; current trades in, 60; seasonal oversupply, 45–46; WWI shortages, 35–36
wheatless days, 142
whiskey, 30–31, 56–59; American Liquor Exchange, 57–59; Whiskey Trust, 56–57
White, E. B., 102
Wilson, James, 53
wine futures, 126–127
Wisconsin, 33, 145
Worker's Magazine, 53
Working Farmer, 29–30
World Development Movement, 164
World Trade Center, 86
World War I: closing of European sugar exchanges during, 84; egg and butter shortages during, 69; and molasses for munitions manufacture, 85; wheat shortage during, 35–36
World War II: government price controls during, 72; and molasses

OKANAGAN REGIONAL LIBRARY
3 3132 03424 7165